from we to
me

EMBRACING LIFE AGAIN AFTER THE
DEATH OR DIVORCE OF A SPOUSE

SUSAN J. ZONNEBELT-SMEENGE, RN, EdD
ROBERT C. DE VRIES, DMin, PhD

BakerBooks

a division of Baker Publishing Group
Grand Rapids, Michigan

© 2010 by Susan J. Zonnebelt-Smeenge and Robert C. De Vries

Published by Baker Books
a division of Baker Publishing Group
P.O. Box 6287, Grand Rapids, MI 49516-6287
www.bakerbooks.com

Printed in the United States of America

Library of Congress Cataloging-in-Publication Data
Zonnebelt-Smeenge, Susan J., 1948-
    From we to me : embracing life again after the death or divorce of a spouse / Susan J. Zonnebelt-Smeenge and Robert C. DeVries.
        p.   cm.
    Includes bibliographical references (p.   ).
    ISBN 978-0-8010-7240-6 (pbk.)
        1. Single people—Religious life. 2. Widows—Religious life. 3. Widowers—Religious life. 4. Divorced people—Religious life. 5. Change—Religious aspects—Christianity. I. DeVries, Robert C., 1942- II. Title.
BV4596.S5Z66 2010
248.8′66—dc22   2010011028

Scripture is taken from the HOLY BIBLE, TODAY'S NEW INTERNATIONAL VERSION®. Copyright © 2001, 2005 by Biblica®. Used by permission of Biblica®. All rights reserved worldwide.

DivorceCare is a network of divorce recovery support group programs. Thousands of groups are meeting worldwide, offering hope, help, and healing to people hurting from separation or divorce. To find a group in your area, visit www.divorcecare.org. If you have children, they will enjoy and find help at DivorceCare for Kids, www.dc4k.org.

GriefShare grief recovery support groups offer comfort, encouragement, and wise counsel to people grieving a death. Group participants discover the strength to walk forward on their journey from mourning to joy. Thousands of these life-changing groups are meeting around the world. Find a nearby group at www.griefshare.org.

10   11   12   13   14   15   16   7   6   5   4   3   2   1

They didn't ask to come on this journey,
but our children and parents,
along with our grandchildren,
have come together into a new
family.

We laugh together,
we pray together,
sometimes we cry together.
So this book is in part a
testimony to the journey
toward blending.

We, therefore, lovingly dedicate this book to:

William and Norma Zonnebelt,
our wonderful parents, who have supported us through the
many challenges;

And our precious children and grandchildren,
Sarah (Zonnebelt-Smeenge) Byrd with her husband Chris
and their children Caleb and Zoe;

Brian De Vries with his wife Marcia;

Christine (De Vries) Hultink with her husband Todd
and their children Hannah and Sophie;

Carrie (De Vries) Geisert with her husband Michael
and their children Elliot, Hayden, and Oliver;

Who have joined us on our journey to become a family
together.

contents

Introduction and Acknowledgments   9

About the Authors   13

1   Moving from We to Me: *Rediscovering Yourself
    through Your Grief Journey*   19
    Understanding Why I Feel So Awful—The Broken Bond   20
    Facing All That's Involved with Grief   23
    Using the Goals of the Grief Process   25
    Becoming Unmarried: What Does It Mean to Be Single?   28
    What Happened to My Self-Esteem?   31
    My Spiritual Journey through Grief   36
        My Faith and Anger Toward God
        Feeling Guilty and Forgiven
        Building Self-esteem God's Way

2   Potholes and Craters: *Filling the Voids When No
    Longer Married*   41
    Are My Friends and Relatives Going to Be There for Me?   42
    What about My Home, Work, and Finances?   46
    Who Will Hug Me Now? Dealing with Touch and Intimacy
        Issues   49

My Spiritual Journey across the Potholes and Craters   51
No Marriage in Heaven
Biblical View of Remarriage
God's Promises about Finances

3 **Deciding to Remain "Me" or Become "We" Again:
   Singleness versus Dating   57**
   Will I or Won't I?   58
   The Choice of Remaining Single   60
   The Pros and Cons of Remaining Single   61
   He/She Is Just a Friend! The Rewards and Consequences of
      Heterosexual Friendships   63
   Deciding to Take the Plunge: Learning to Date in a Different
      World   64
   The Three *P*s Regarding Dating: Precautions, Protocols, and
      Possibilities   68
   My Spiritual Journey in Finding "Me"   74
   Remaining Single
   Making Decisions about My Life
   Sexuality while Single

4 **The Second Time Around: *Things You Need to Know
   about Dating and Remarriage*   79**
   Lessons Learned from Before   80
   Six Things to Assess as You Deal with Your Past When
      Seriously Dating Each Other   83
   Seven Things to Talk Through before You Say "I Do"   86
   My Spiritual Journey in Considering Dating and
      Remarriage   95
   Loving Again
   Marrying a Non-Christian

5 **In Our Own Words: *A Sequel to "The Second Time
   Around"*   99**
   Through Our Eyes as Widowed   99
   Susan and Bob's Perspectives on Dating and Remarriage
   Their Kids' Perspectives on Dating and Remarriage
   Through the Eyes of the Divorced   110
   Jean and Ed's Perspectives on Dating and Remarriage
   Their Kids' Perspectives on Dating and Remarriage

6 Blended or Chunky: *The Art of Parenting and Stepparenting* 121

  Part 1: Observations about Blending a Chunky Family 122

  Some Suggestions for the Road Ahead—Blended or Chunky 122

  What Can I Do as the New Stepparent to Begin This Blending Process in a Positive Way? 123

  How Will I Parent My Children, My Partner's Children, and Our Joint Children? 125

  What Will the Kids Call Me as Their Stepparent? 126

  Part 2: Blending a Chunky Family with Young Children in the Home 127

  Who Sets and Enforces the Rules for Dependent Children? 127

  What Role Does My Ex-spouse Play in Raising the Children? 129

  Part 3: Blending a Chunky Family with Emerging or Established Adult Children 130

  My Spiritual Journey While Parenting and Stepparenting 134

   Being Family Together

   Healthy (Step)parenting

   Managing Resistance

7 In Our Own Words: *A Sequel to "Blended or Chunky"* 141

  Through Our Eyes as Widowed 141

   Susan and Bob's Perspectives on Blending Their Families

   Their Kids' Perspectives on Blending Their Families

  Through the Eyes of the Divorced 152

   Jean and Ed's Perspectives on Blending Their Families

   Their Kids' Perspectives on Blending Their Families

8 Embracing Your Past—Empowering Your Future: *The Art of Moving On* 161

  Preparing for the Next Chapter 162

  Being Deliberate about Learning from Your Personal Experiences 164

  Setting New Goals for Your Life 166

  My Spiritual Journey to Embrace and Empower 170

   Facing Your Future

Notes 174

introduction and acknowledgments

This is the fifth book we have written together since our first spouses died. In our writing and speaking, we present both the psychological and spiritual perspectives on the issues at hand. Three of our books deal with grief following a loved one's death; two of those are for all relationships and one specifically for a surviving spouse. Another book deals with preparing for one's death whether young and healthy or older and ill.

This latest book ventures into some new territory for us in that we are speaking with those who have experienced the loss of a spouse not only through death but through a divorce as well. The primary issues under consideration are how a person redefines himself or herself and reinvests in life in a way that becomes fulfilling and rewarding. Invariably those challenges eventually give rise to the question of whether or not a person wants to begin dating. For some people, remaining single is the preferred option, so we deal with how to fully embrace that lifestyle when your marriage ends. Others may want to date, and from that perhaps enter into another close relationship, and possibly remarry. And if one does remarry we discuss how to blend families in a healthy way.

We want to acknowledge the role that our children and Susan's parents have played in birthing this book. This is our collective experience—for better and sometimes for worse. All of us have attempted to be candid about coming together as a new family. The journey continues even after thirteen wonderfully amazing years of marriage to each other.

We also want to acknowledge our close personal friends whom (wishing to remain anonymous) we call Ed and Jean in this book, and who married each other after both being divorced. They, along with their children (also using pseudonyms), participated in giving shape and a rich substance to this work. Their story is real, challenging, and hopeful.

We appreciate as well the comments in reviewing our manuscript given by our good friends, Doug and Carol Luther. They have also walked the widowed journey and developed a life together after that.

We also want to acknowledge the several hundred people who have participated in the Younger Widowed Support Group through Greater Grand Rapids Widowed Persons Services (MI) that we have facilitated for the past twelve years. We have seen so many of them enter the group filled with grief, fear, and anxiety over the shape of their future only to emerge a year to three years later invigorated by the possibilities of their new life.

We would be remiss if we did not also recognize the dedicated staff of Baker Publishing Group who have provided us with tremendous support and encouragement ever since we began publishing with them in 1998. We especially want to thank Robert Hosack, senior acquisitions editor, with whom we share our visions, dreams, and sometimes frustrations. His faith in our writing and speaking on these topics is greatly appreciated. We also thank Kristin Kornoelje, assistant managing editor of trade books, for helping to give clear voice to our writing.

This book is a testimony to the fact that you *can* get through your grief after the death or divorce of your spouse. Our hope is that this book will also provide you with valuable information and insights for you to use on your journey toward embracing life fully once again after the significant, life-changing loss of your spouse.

Susan J. Zonnebelt-Smeenge, RN, EdD
Robert C. De Vries, DMin, PhD

about the authors

This book had a thirteen-year gestation period, beginning with our marriage in 1997 and reaching its publication in 2010. We had received numerous requests to write something for those emerging from grief and facing their future. However, we really wanted to include the whole gamut of possibilities and so needed more experience with our own blending in order to write about this topic. We have now walked the road from being widowed, to embracing a single lifestyle, to dating, and then to marrying each other and working at blending our families. Since this book contains so much of our heart and soul, we thought you might benefit from knowing a little more about each of us before you begin reading.

Susan J. Zonnebelt-Smeenge, RN, EdD, is a licensed clinical psychologist at Pine Rest Christian Mental Health Services in Grand Rapids, Michigan. She began her professional life as a registered nurse, eventually teaching nursing. But when her husband, Rick, was diagnosed with a malignant brain tumor at the age of thirty, she decided to pursue a doctoral program to become a licensed clinical psychologist in order to provide better stability and financial support for herself, her husband, and their daughter. Rick, who had received multiple prognoses of short-term survival, lived for almost eighteen years, dying in 1994 after twenty-four years of marriage. By then, Susan was forty-six years old, and their daughter Sarah, at the age of eighteen, had just entered college. Rick and Susan never had other children because of the radiation Rick received and his terminal diagnosis.

Robert C. De Vries, DMin, PhD, is an ordained minister in the Christian Reformed Church of North America, a denomination of approximately two hundred thousand members, located primarily in the northern and western regions of the United States and in Canada. His wife, Char, developed ovarian cancer at the age of forty-seven and died three and a half years later in 1993 after twenty-eight years of marriage. Bob was fifty-one years old at the time. They had three children—Brian, Christy, and Carrie—all of whom were emerging adults at the time of their mother's death.

We met each other as professional colleagues seven months after Rick's death. We wanted to explore how to deal with the challenge of being caregivers in our professions while working through our own loss issues. We soon decided that we shared enough interest, experience, and expertise in the area of dying and grieving that we could collaborate on a book designed to help those who had also experienced the death of a spouse. After completing the manuscript we discovered there might be more to our relationship, and, as one reporter commented, "Somewhere along the line, romance tiptoed in." The book, *Getting to the Other Side of Grief: Overcoming the Loss of a Spouse*, was published in 1998 and continues to be available in English, Spanish, French, and Dutch.

Our writing, speaking, and consulting on dying and grief issues continued to grow. We wrote a book entitled *The Empty Chair: Handling Grief on Holidays and Special Occasions* to help families deal with grief at those times of the year when they especially feel the absence of a deceased loved one. *Living Fully in the Shadow of Death: Assurance and Guidance to Finish Well* was our next project. As care-providers to our first spouses, we learned the critical importance of helping people prepare for their own death when they are still healthy, when they face a potentially terminal illness, and/or when death is imminent. We returned our focus to the grief journey with the publication of *Traveling through Grief: Learning to Live Again After the Death of a Loved One.* We believe there are five goals a grieving person must intentionally pursue in grieving the death of a loved one, so in that book we outline a number of specific activities and behaviors that help people deliberately work on their grief rather than merely (and ineffectively) waiting for grief to rectify itself.

This current book, *From We to Me*, chronicles the numerous choices a person has to make following the loss of a spouse. The book expands on our prior writing in that we now include loss through both death and divorce. We believe that many of the issues of redefining oneself and reinvesting in life find significant parallels in these two groups of people. Questions such as "Who am I now?" "What kind of lifestyle do I want to develop?" "Do I want to remain single or begin dating?" "If I do date, do I really want to get into a serious relationship or should I keep my dating on a social level?" "If I do get serious about another relationship, what do I need to know and do if I want to move toward getting married again?" And, "If I do get married again, what is involved in blending the two families?"

We try to give direction in these areas, but at times we simply tell our story and let you find yourself at various points in the narrative. Our story is ongoing. The passing of another five or ten years may shed even more light on our perspective on blending. But given our experience, our professional insight, and our work together for more than a decade in the field of grief and loss education and consulting, we hope that our words will provide the help and direction you are seeking as you move from "we" to "me" following the death or divorce of your spouse.

One final comment about the title is in order. *From We to Me* may imply, on the surface, that the book deals only with remaining single. That is not the case. We deal with remaining single, dating, remarriage, and blending. But the "me" remains the key even for developing a healthy remarriage. Especially if you married young the first time, you likely did not know yourself the way you do now. You did not have the same rich life experiences. Knowing the "me" you have become will be a healthy asset if you do decide to become a "we" again. But you can only make the choice in a healthy way when you truly "know yourself."

Sunrise

Ruby rays erode the dark night.
Silently, persistently, the light trickles
brighter
higher
illuminating flowers and faults alike.
Challenges of yesterday intercourse with
promises of tomorrow
today.
You begin again, again.
Sunrise.

1

moving from we to me

Rediscovering Yourself
through Your Grief Journey

Amanda's Journal: My friend Marilyn helped me today. "Like a tapestry that was woven together," she said, "that's what marriage is like. How do you expect to suddenly feel good about yourself when that tapestry has been ripped in half? The edges are all rough and tattered." "Exactly!" I thought. I met Gary in high school. We dated for eight years. We grew up together. We celebrated our twenty-fifth anniversary. Now he's dead, and my life looks dark! And I'm supposed to have a future? We were a future together. I don't even know what I want, much less know how to go about getting there.

Josh's Journal: I've made a mess of my life—that's for sure. She moved out six months ago. I thought I would feel relieved and happy. After all, she didn't want to be married anymore. I feel so confused and afraid. Oh, I see her every once in a while—picking up the kids, at school plays, and the like—but we're no longer a couple. I am really on my own. I didn't think it would be this hard. All the decisions. Everyone else seems to have a future, but I can hardly see far enough ahead to plan dinner for the kids.

Understanding Why I Feel So Awful—The Broken Bond

It happened! Something none of us ever wanted to face. Loss—significant loss. You may lose many important things over your lifetime, but nothing compares with the loss of your spouse. At the marriage altar, you vowed to live with this person for the rest of your earthly life. You believed your marriage would be happy and fulfilling. Then the marriage came to an end. Whether it was through a death or divorce, you never intended this to happen.

The loss of your marriage felt awful, didn't it? After developing a deep attachment to your spouse and then having your relationship end, the pain can be intense. Your two lives that were intertwined are separated. The hurt felt like a knife piercing the flesh of your heart. The emotional and physical intimacy you may once have had with your kindred spirit, lover, and best friend is over. Grief is overwhelming as you realize that all your hopes, dreams, plans, and promises are gone—totally wiped out, never to come true in the ways you had imagined.

Words for the Widowed

Most of us hate the word *dead* because it names the unspeakable. You probably thought this wouldn't happen to you, at least not until you were very old—or you thought that you might just die together. Your spouse was always going to be the other half of what made you feel whole. Widowed people often say they feel incomplete, like they are only "half a person." That feeling usually lasts quite a while. This book is about how you can grow to feel whole again without your beloved partner.

"I didn't want this to happen; I didn't deserve it!" is the cry of many widowed people recognizing their helplessness to prevent the death. If your marriage was happy and fulfilling, you likely are grateful for the time you had together. But often that makes the pain of grief even sharper and more intense for a while. Even so, you may have a number of regrets—regretting that you can't fulfill your joint dreams, go places you wanted to go as a couple, and simply enjoy growing old together.

While other people may have some compassion for you, they will not necessarily be there when you want help or understand what you are going through. But at least they will not blame you for what happened, and hopefully they will be compassionate and empathetic. On the other hand, some people may withdraw from you, feeling inadequate to deal with what has happened, or they may subconsciously fear that their spouse may die too. Being supported by others is definitely helpful, but this is still your personal journey, and you are the only one who can get yourself through it.

We use the journey metaphor because dealing with the loss of your spouse is a process that takes time. Grieving also takes hard work to find your bearings again and to feel like you are a valuable, though single, person. But if you continue to put forth the effort and give yourself time, you can eventually heal and feel whole again.

Words for the Divorced

Divorced—the word sounds ugly, doesn't it? No one gets married wanting the marriage to fail. But two people who were once allies have become adversaries divided now in a multitude of ways. Other people may think you could have avoided the divorce. Perhaps you might have. But maybe not. Perhaps you are devastated because you didn't want the divorce and still in some ways love your spouse. Maybe you wanted to try counseling, but your spouse decided to end the marriage without working on the problems. Of course, when one person resists a reconciliation, the marriage can't survive. It takes two to make a healthy marriage.

On the other hand, you may feel victimized because the marriage wasn't a healthy place for you, so you filed for divorce out of self-defense. Did you get to the point where you couldn't live with the physical or emotional abuse, the infidelity, or some addiction? Or did you feel so insignificant and emotionally battered that you finally had to say you had enough? That's often such a difficult choice to end your marriage but ultimately a healthy one. Hopefully that means you valued yourself enough to terminate a relationship that was disgraceful and detrimental after first doing what you could to change it.

Then again, you may be the one who violated your marital vows. Your love may have grown cold, you had an affair, immersed yourself in work, or struggled with an addiction (like gambling, substances, or porn) that eventually shattered the marriage. Some people erroneously think that as the initiator of the divorce you won't grieve the end of your marriage. But we think that no one ever walks down the marriage aisle wanting it to someday end. Brides and grooms typically dream of a wonderful life together. You probably included "till death do us part" in your wedding vows, and now your divorce scoffs at that promise. So you grieve your failed promise as well as the end of your joint hopes and dreams.

In either case, as the recipient or initiator of the divorce, you now grieve whatever you lost. No one wins in a divorce. Together you were unsuccessful in keeping the marriage intact, and so now you may feel guilty, shamed, or as though you failed. Your grief journey will be unique depending on your personal circumstances but nevertheless difficult because a vow that was intended to last a lifetime was broken.

Facing All That's Involved with Grief

Grief descended like a cloud when your spouse died or when she or he walked out the door. Your life seemed empty and hopeless. You may still have a hard time some days believing this has happened to you. The reality of your loss creeps into your consciousness in bits and pieces as you try to get the children off to school, balance the checkbook with only your income, and then exhausted crawl solo into a cold, uninviting bed to fight the awful loneliness that presses in on you.

You have most likely already discovered that the grief you are experiencing is composed of a number of different components. For example, grief affects the way you *think*, making healthy decisions extremely difficult. Your normal *behaviors* will be affected, especially your memory, concentration, and motivation. Grief will affect you *physically*, with exhaustion as one of the biggest culprits. If all of this weren't enough, significant loss forces you to try to make sense out of the devastation you have experienced. You likely cry out, "Why me?" and "Why now?" which often leads to deeper *spiritual* searching. Of course, the *emotional* component of grief is always pressing on you. You likely experience a number of conflicting feelings ranging from sadness and hurt to anger, guilt, regret, and often relief as well. Feelings are a big part of what makes you a distinct person. Coupled with your thoughts, beliefs, and values, they contribute to your uniqueness. What you *feel* isn't right or wrong, good or bad. Feelings just *are*. It's what you do with your feelings that makes your behavior either healthy or unhealthy. Feelings change over time, especially as you begin to work through them and formulate new thoughts and behaviors. So be careful not to stuff or avoid your feelings, because that can lead to other physical or emotional problems down the road. Feelings don't go away on their own; they need to be dealt with openly and honestly.

Getting through your grief with all of these components (your thoughts, behaviors, physical symptoms, spiritual questioning, and emotional responses) takes time—at the very least a minimum of one year but more often two to four years. Taking time to grieve is essential to your healing, but you also need to intentionally work at five goals of grief, which we will describe in the following section.

Words for the Widowed

No feelings are inappropriate when your partner has died, although some feelings may be embarrassing or make you wonder if you're going crazy. Most widowed people feel intense pain at the death of their spouse, often coupled with anxiety, emptiness, regret, and fear to name just a few. On the other hand, you may have been considering divorcing your spouse before he or she died. Not all marriages were healthy and happy. If that was your situation, your sadness may be laced with a number of other negative feelings. Whether your marriage was healthy or unhealthy, happy or unhappy, or somewhere in between, you will experience both positive and negative emotions. That is normal. We urge you to find healthy outlets for your emotions through things like journaling, letter writing, crying, getting physical exercise, screaming or wailing in private.

Words for the Divorced

As a divorced person, you may find that dealing with your emotions demands a lot of your attention. If your spouse initiated the divorce, you may feel helpless because this wasn't something you wanted. Working through your emotions of hurt and anger takes time and intentional work so that bitterness doesn't take hold of you. If you initiated the divorce, you may feel guilty for leaving your former partner in the lurch. If dependent children are involved, you may be concerned about the effects the divorce will have on them. You may have anxiety over custody issues or how much time will be allotted to you for parenting your children. Because divorce is often unwanted and feels disgraceful, other people aren't typically too compassionate and may offer little support to either party, which can be hurtful and a challenge to handle.

Using the Goals of the Grief Process

How you view what has happened to you with your spouse's death or divorce is going to influence the outcome of your grief journey. If you can accept the reality of the loss even though you did not want it, you are laying a healthy foundation for healing. Although grieving is a unique individual journey, we believe everyone needs to work on five interactive and nonsequential goals in order to get through grieving the loss of their spouse. These, we think, are essential for your healing whether you were widowed or divorced. We will mention them all briefly here but will focus on only two of them in this book. You can read in detail about the other three goals in one of the books we coauthored, *Traveling through Grief: Learning to Live Again after the Death of a Loved One*.[1] In that book you will find numerous examples of specific ways to work on each of these goals of grieving. The purpose of this book you are now reading is to help you deal more specifically with the two of these five goals that have to do with the "me" you are rediscovering. They are to:

- Learn to identify who you are now, independent of the relationship you had with your previous spouse.
- Reinvest fully in life, creating a "new normal" that is rich, full, and satisfying—whether you remain single or later remarry.

The other three goals that are not the focus here, but are equally important to work through, are to:

- Accept the reality of the death or divorce of your spouse.

- Express all the emotions associated with this significant loss.

- Learn to store the memories of your life with your previous spouse, moving that relationship into the past while being able to recall memories free of the initial pain and hurt associated with the death or divorce.

Two words, *intentional* and *active*, are critical to your approach in achieving these goals of grieving. Be *intentional* about grieving when you have the motivation and energy to *actively* engage in specific behaviors to achieve these goals. That means you will have many things you will need to do and face in order to work through your grief.

Your grief journey will undoubtedly have its ups and downs, its joys and sorrows. Recognizing that life is a combination of both joy and sadness helps you gain a more realistic picture of what has happened. Nothing is perfect or lasts forever. Life is a continual process filled with dynamic change. You have experienced a profound and unwanted change with your loss. Now you need to work through your grief by taking hold of your pain and working through it to the point where you no longer feel the intense, heart-piercing sadness of your loss. Hold firmly to the belief that you are going to survive this most unfortunate event in your life, and you will become stronger and wiser as a result.

When you have reached the end of your grieving and are ready to embark on a new course for your life, make certain you have completed all the goals of grieving, have removed the wedding ring from your fourth finger (having done something else with it), and have said a final good-bye to your previous spouse. Good-bye is difficult to say, particularly if you didn't want your marriage to end. You will say it hundreds of times to all the various aspects of the life you shared with your spouse that are no more. You will realize it each time you do something new without your previous spouse. And one day you will know it's time to say the final good-bye. That does take an intentional decision on your part. It helps to do it in a symbolic, meaningful way such as writing a special letter, doing a balloon launch, or using some other type of ceremony. Then you are ready to face an exciting new beginning for yourself that has already started to become your "new normal." Hopefully this "new normal" will encompass and reflect all the growth you achieved in working through your grief journey.

Words for the Widowed

As time goes by, hopefully you are accepting the reality that your partner died, that he or she will no longer walk the face of this earth. For a while, you may have thought you caught a glimpse of your deceased spouse or heard his or her voice. That is perfectly normal. But gradually you realize that your spouse really is no longer present and will never use any of his or her belongings again. So you need to decide what you want to do with them. This process is painful because it signifies an important step on your grief journey dealing with accepting the reality of your spouse's death.

We would caution you, as you recall fond memories of your life with your partner, to keep those memories balanced. You will certainly want to remember all the good times, but don't overlook those times that were frustrating or irritating. Some people get stymied thinking that remembering these negative aspects is being disloyal, sacrilegious, or unfair to someone who can no longer defend himself or herself. But actually that is being realistic and honest. Nobody's marriage was perfect because no person is without some faults or shortcomings. If you don't work toward remembering your relationship realistically, your grief journey will be more complicated and prolonged, and sadly, you may not be able to adequately proceed through grieving to get to the other side.

Words for the Divorced

As a divorced person, you have to deal with the fact that although your former spouse is still alive, you are no longer partnered with him or her. In fact, you likely separated all ties with that person except for provisions in the divorce settlement regarding minor children. If you had children together, you need to decide how you and your ex-spouse will cooperate in providing for their needs. If you didn't want the divorce and still love your spouse, building your new life without that person may be especially challenging. You will need to work through letting go of your previous partner. How will you respond if your ex-spouse shows up unexpectedly at an event? Or how will you feel if your former partner begins a new relationship with someone else? You need to address all your feelings and accept the difficult realities that accompany divorce so you no longer desire that previous relationship and can move toward healing. If you intensely dislike your ex-spouse now because of all the hurt and turmoil of the divorce, you won't do yourself any favors by remaining bitter and angry. While the process of forgiveness may be difficult, learning to work through your intense feelings so they no longer have power is worth the effort in the long run.

Becoming Unmarried: What Does It Mean to Be Single?

You may never have thought about being single again, especially if you viewed being married as the ultimate, preferred status for you. There are many people who can't imagine being unmarried, and others who view singleness as only a temporary state of affairs.

To most married people, everyone else seems to be married as well. However, do you realize that about half of the adult US population is single? That comes as a surprise to many, probably because when married we tend to surround ourselves primarily with other married couples rather than those who are single. So when your marriage ended, you probably didn't have many single friends. As you work through your grief, you will need to work on accepting that you are again single. You will need to deal with this as you move from "we" to "me."

Being single has both *positive* and *negative* aspects to it. From the *negative* perspective, you no longer have one special person who is supposed to care about the details of your life, nor do you have someone with whom you can be intimate. You need to make decisions by yourself and are solely responsible for each outcome whether good or bad. You have no kindred spirit with whom to set goals and plan for the future. On the *positive* side, you can make your own decisions without having to consider someone else's desires or feelings. You don't have to accommodate another person with regard to spending patterns, relationships with children, vacation choices, social or recreational activities, or anything else.

You have moved from being married to either widowed or divorced. As you emerge from grieving, hopefully you can embrace yourself as a single person. While being single may at first seem to be quite negative, hopefully you will be able to see that setting your own life course and pursuing your passions can be a positive and exhilarating opportunity unencumbered by someone else who may have different ideas, wants, and needs. Learn ways to make being single a positive experience so you can embrace your new life as a single person.

Words for the Widowed

Being widowed isn't a label you wanted, yet no word sounds good to denote the fact your spouse died or to capture the devastation you feel following his or her death. An accident, a medically caused sudden death, or a lengthy illness involving your spouse are horrid events to have to experience. Now you are left to figure out how to adjust to a life without that person's presence, help, and support.

On your wedding day you vowed to love each other until one of you died. The harsh reality is that death has ended your marriage. You are no longer married. You need to unweave your marital threads to see who you are now without your spouse. As you heal from grieving it is healthy to become more comfortable calling yourself "single." That doesn't mean you can't explain your singleness by stating you were widowed. You may not yet believe that you can build a rich and rewarding life as a single person, but your challenge is to discover ways to do just that in order to move from "we" to "me" in healthy ways.

Words for the Divorced

After being divorced, you may feel very strange being single. You might sense other people's negative judgment that you couldn't keep your marriage intact and as a result feel embarrassed or inadequate. None of us likes to fail, especially when we valued our marriage and knew it was important. However, something most likely happened that damaged the marriage, creating more distance in your relationship over issues that could not be adequately resolved. If you were the one who initiated the divorce, being single might sound preferable to you, better than being shackled in a marriage that had reached a dead end. On the other hand, if your partner was the one to file for the divorce, you may be facing quite a different story. You may have wanted to put more effort into trying to repair the marriage, thinking there was still some worth in your union. So changing your status from married to divorced is difficult enough, much less beginning to think of yourself as single. But hang in there, this is part of the journey. We think you'll realize that being single might actually turn out to have some positives to offer, and you'll be able to find things to enjoy about that status.

30

What Happened to My Self-Esteem?

To other people, the movement from being widowed or divorced to being single may seem rather automatic. However, they don't understand the internal struggle you face trying to redefine yourself once you are no longer partnered. As much as some people may radiate genuine caring and empathetically try to understand, none of them is you. Their help can only go so far. As a widowed or divorced person, only you can figure out who you really are now as you adjust to flying solo.

We are talking about your *self-image* (how you *see* yourself), *self-concept* (how you *think* about yourself), and *self-esteem* (how you *value* yourself). These three components constitute the essence of who you are and how you relate to others. They are also deeply affected by how you think others see you and how, if you are a religious person, you think God sees you.

The loss of your partner has a dramatic impact on your self-esteem, raising a multitude of questions: Who am I now without my spouse? What value can I possibly have by myself? How can I see myself positively? These questions are often accompanied by higher levels of self-doubt and misgivings. Marriage usually helps increase a person's self-esteem. In a healthy marriage your partner affirms you; you are valuable to him or her. When that relationship is gone, the temptation is to think that you are no longer valuable, capable, or desirable. You need to be very intentional about reminding yourself that you, as an individual, have your own intrinsic value and worth. You were a valuable and important person before your marriage. Even in your marriage, whether it was healthy or not, you were still an important individual with your own skills, ideas, beliefs, and perspectives. Through the process of rediscovering yourself as a single person, hopefully you will be able to again see yourself as significant and worthwhile.

If you have not already done so, focus on developing or recommitting yourself to a pattern of healthy self-care so that you will have more energy and stamina for the challenges ahead. The grief journey can be exhausting if you don't take care of yourself and deliberately pace your daily schedule. Good self-care validates that you really do matter both to yourself and to others. So we encourage you to incorporate the three foundational ingredients essential to physical and mental health: eat, sleep, and exercise. Start small, but do begin! You need to make certain you are eating three-plus healthy meals a day even if you haven't felt like it. Some people think that cooking for one is no fun. Cooking alone can be enjoyable; you *are* as valuable as your partner was. Don't fall into the trap of saying "it's only for me." It *is* you, and you do matter. Get adequate sleep (an average of eight hours per night), but don't use sleep to avoid grieving by taking lengthy naps or oversleeping. Get the regular physical exercise you need to keep fit. We suggest an exercise or a walking program that you can do at least four times a week, building up to a minimum of thirty minutes each time. Buy a pedometer and challenge yourself to try for ten thousand steps a day. You'll begin to have more energy and feel more in control of your life when you attend to these three necessary components.

We would also encourage you to maintain good personal hygiene and pay attention to your appearance. In light of the magnitude of your loss, we understand that you might think these things are unimportant. But taking good care of your body and your appearance does wonders for your self-esteem. Seeing your physician for a physical exam after a spousal death or divorce is imperative. You may not have been taking very good care of yourself with all that had been transpiring in your life. After a spousal loss your health automatically becomes more at risk because of the negative stressors you have experienced. Discuss your dietary, sleep, and mood issues with your doctor. At first you may not be highly motivated to do any of these things, but taking care of yourself will be less difficult as you begin to develop a better sense of well-being.

Liking yourself and believing you are a good person are critical for your journey. If you had positive self-esteem before your spouse died or you divorced, you are at an advantage in your efforts to regain a sense of value and worth. A sense of self-esteem originally develops at a young age through developmental successes and the affirmation of others. If you had a secure, affirming, and loving childhood filled with praise and positive reinforcement, you likely have a solid foundation on which to build. On the other hand, if your self-esteem was somewhat low prior to your spouse's death or the divorce, the impact of that severe crisis on your sense of self may be greater. By all means, don't let other people's negative comments, criticisms, or judgments define you. Don't be excessively concerned about what other people may think of you—that gives them far too much power. Remember, we may have different ideas, beliefs, abilities, and skills, but we are all of equal value. You control your own choices, so make them in a way that guards your integrity.

We would also suggest you compliment yourself by saying things like "Good going—that turned out well," "You look so nice in that outfit," "You certainly are a very caring person," or "Good job for exercising." Tune into what you say to yourself throughout the day. In spite of the jokes about talking to yourself, positive self-talk is healthy and normal. The internal conversations you have with yourself throughout the day most likely contain both positive and negative messages. If you are critical of yourself and put yourself down, you may be repeating messages you have heard at an earlier time in your life that are destructive to your sense of self. Try earnestly to reframe those messages since they usually do not represent who you really are and do damage to your self-esteem. We know that no one is perfect and that everyone makes mistakes. Trust that the more you can be positive and affirming of yourself, the more secure and confident you will feel, and your sense of value and worth will grow stronger.

Use this time of rebuilding to engage in some of the activities and interests you may have had before or always wanted to try. Do some new things a few times before deciding if you'll want to add them to your repertoire. It's the process of discovering the "me" emerging from the "we" of your former life.

Maybe you rarely did things by yourself, whether it was shopping, eating out, going to social events or movies, or spending an overnight or weekend by yourself. Being intentionally alone might sound unappealing to you because now you are often alone but not by your choice. You will need to accept that living alone (without your previous partner) is now the reality of your life. In time you may even find that it is preferable to many other situations you could be in. Remember, being alone doesn't have to mean you are lonely; alone and lonely are really two different things. You can be alone and not feel lonely. At other times you can be in a room full of people and still feel terribly lonely. The more you do by yourself, the better you will feel about yourself. Believe it or not, you can actually get to the point (again) of feeling that you are your own best friend. We hope you develop the capacity to like yourself and at times actually prefer being alone and doing things by yourself. You can be good company for yourself and have the confidence to go anywhere and do anything you want by yourself.

One final word is in order. To feel valuable and worthwhile, you will want to identify your longer-term purposes as you step out of your grief into a whole new world. How will you now be involved in and contribute to the world around you? Many times people define themselves by what they "do"—by their careers or volunteer efforts. Doing those things is, of course, important, but you will miss the mark if you don't also consider your "being." One's life purposes also include developing your values and beliefs as well as your personality—all that makes up who you "are," not just what you "do." You are a one-of-a-kind person with distinct purposes, gifts, and perspectives. Go forward to both "be" and "do" as you enter this new phase of your life.

Words for the Widowed

Probably most of the people you know, including your family, friends, business associates, and church family, thought of you and your partner as a couple. You were connected and joined together. The things you both valued, believed, and participated in were largely harmonic. People likely at times referred to you as "Mary and Harry" rather than just one or the other of you. "You" became plural—"me" became "we." In a healthy marriage, your partner cared deeply for you, listened to you, and affirmed you, told you that you were beautiful or handsome, and that you were talented and had a great personality. Your spouse liked most everything about you. He or she would hold you when you were hurt and support you when you faced difficulties. The unique kind of belief your partner had in you helped increase and enhance your self-esteem. So you grieved heartily because you would no longer hear those compliments and feel that approval. However, if your marriage was conflictual or had other serious problems, now you probably have to contend all the more with the impact of both your past marital relationship and your spouse's death on your self-esteem.

Words for the Divorced

When a person is divorced, either the divorce happened by mutual consent or one person took the initiative and the other was forced to respond to the decision of their partner. If the divorce was by mutual consent, a person's self-esteem may not be as deeply affected as it might be in a contested divorce. But in either case, you still need to go through the redefinition process from "we" to "me."

If you find yourself struggling to accept a divorce you did not want, your self-esteem may be jolted and considerably lower than it was when you entered the marriage. Divorce spells rejection, being "unwanted" goods and no longer valuable to your partner. You may have been the focus of all kinds of accusations since divorce is the epitome of a personal attack. "She was such a nag" or "He was never home—so unfeeling and unavailable." "She was as cold as a fish—never interested in sex" or "He was such an animal—making demands of me verbally in front of the kids." Arguments and accusations fly back and forth. Little wonder that your self-esteem took a hit. All the hurt, anger, and rejection leads to a sense of insecurity and inadequacy that plays havoc with your ability to like who you are and feel worthwhile. You will have to work hard to reframe all those negative accusations and discern if there might be some truth in them that you would benefit from looking at.

If you were the one who initiated the divorce, you may have felt the relationship was no longer reciprocal or fulfilling, or you already developed what you thought was a more satisfying relationship with someone else. You will need to ask how you feel about yourself now in light of your role in the marital breakup. Undoubtedly that will have some impact on your self-esteem. You may be asking: How do I get to the point of liking myself again when I feel so guilty? Can I ever forgive myself, or be forgiven, for what I have done? We certainly believe you can forgive yourself and be forgiven. You need to evaluate if and how your values and perspectives changed in order to determine where they need to be for you to feel good about yourself again. Only as you deal with all of your emotions and face these issues squarely will you be able to move on in life with a repaired self-esteem.

my spiritual journey through grief

Why did God let this happen to me? Was my faith not strong enough? What can I do with my feelings of anger toward God and toward my spouse?

Holding God responsible for the bad things that happen in life is a common reaction, especially when your spouse has died or your marriage has failed. Spiritually most of us believe that God is loving and kind, so we like to think that means he won't let bad things happen to us. Starry-eyed at the wedding altar, we subconsciously believe life will be perfect—nothing will happen to upset the joy we feel on our wedding day. But that's the problem. We do not live in a perfect world, and no marriage is perfect either. Arguments arise; disloyalty happens; disease strikes; divorce and death occur. One or the other will end every marriage. Evil is a reality. You have to face the fact that evil has taken on a particularly personal form in the death or divorce of your spouse. The strength of your faith really has very little to do with why this happened, but it has everything to do with how you will continue to manage it. Hopefully by now you are eager to begin reshaping and redefining your future. But that future is very uncertain. Isn't that what faith is really all about—believing that with God's help and your resolve, you can move ahead even when things look so unclear and uncertain?

It's also quite possible that you may have some feelings of anger toward God. When these negative feelings surface, you may be embarrassed, feel guilty, or fear that God will get angry with you in return. Do know God can handle your anger toward him. But consider this: your anger may not be anger with God at all but rather anger that this death or divorce happened in your life. You may still think that God could have done something about it but didn't choose to prevent it from happening. However, the Christian faith accepts the fact that God isn't going to fix every broken relationship on earth. God allows (does not interfere with) the natural consequences that come because of the broken condition of this world.

Here's another factor you might consider: God is actually angry along with you—not at you, but with you. He is angry about this brokenness as well. After all, this world was his beautiful creation, and now it's all messed up. He doesn't like death or divorce; that's why he sent his Son Jesus to fix it. And that final redemption is still coming. But for now, we live with the brokenness. So when you feel angry at God for the brokenness you experience in the loss of your partner, remind yourself that he is actually angry along with you at the evil that caused your pain. And he's still doing something about it.

Why do I feel so guilty? Was it my fault? Can I forgive myself? And will God?

"But," you may respond, "I feel so guilty. I think I could have avoided this divorce or prevented my spouse's death. If only I had done something differently, this might not have happened." Feeling guilty is a common reaction to the situation you find yourself in. The problem is that you can't turn back the clock. Even if you genuinely believe that having done something differently might have changed the outcome, the fact is that you already did what you did. Remember, hindsight is 20/20. Just be satisfied knowing you did what you thought best at the time you made your decision. This is where forgiveness comes into play—especially understand that God does forgive you, and then have the confidence that you can forgive yourself. Once you believe God has forgiven you, refusing to forgive yourself is a slap in God's face because he is perfect and above sin, yet he will forgive you. The journey toward healing is a spiritual journey of accepting that you have limitations and make mistakes but also can forgive yourself though God's example of forgiveness. Then live fully in that forgiveness as a new person. What may look like a totally devastating event in your life right now can become the seed of your new life. But the journey begins with learning to forgive yourself just as God forgives you.

Is self-esteem something I should work on as a Christian? I thought I was supposed to be humble and meek.

A number of years ago a breakfast food company ran an advertisement for a cereal that had initially been marketed to adults. In an attempt to broaden its appeal to include children, they featured a young boy enthusiastically eating the cereal while his friend who was watching declared: "Mikey likes it! He really likes it!" His friend then proceeded to get a bowl and pour himself some. If someone we are close to likes something, we tend to be more open to trying it and probably liking it ourselves. In some interesting way, this may shed light on a Christian understanding of self-esteem.

Many Christians have been brought up with phrases such as "Christ must increase and I must decrease," or "I am unworthy and a sinner." These phrases are biblically correct. It is true that Christ must increase in our lives, and outside of Christ, we are in fact sinners! So because that focus is negative, we tend to put ourselves down. But that's not the end of the story. The literal "good news" is that God loved us in Christ with an eternal and redeeming love, and we are worthy through him.

We'd like to suggest three aspects of how Christ's love for us provides the foundation for a Christian understanding of self-esteem.

First, Christian self-esteem begins with loving what God loves. If Mikey liked the cereal, hopefully his friend would too. Isn't it much more true that if we are in Christ, and God likes something, we will like it too? And guess what! God loves you. That may be hard to believe, especially if you have recently experienced the rejection of a divorce or abandonment through your spouse's death. You may feel unlovable. Then remind yourself that there is no love in the entire universe greater than God's love for you in Jesus Christ. While that will not exempt you from the pain of grief, hopefully meditating on God's love for you in Christ will help you remember that ultimately you are a treasure in God's eyes.

Second, focus on what you are becoming, not on what you have been. You may presently feel abandoned, lost, or broken. You are once again unmarried, "single," feeling quite alone in this world. But now is the time to remind yourself that God will not abandon you. He has purposes for your life that go well beyond a partnered relationship. Not only does he encourage you to stay on the journey, but he also promises that he will be your guide and your strength through his Spirit. Nothing will be able to separate you from his love, not even the death or divorce of your spouse.

Third, embrace your uniqueness. You are an individual creation of God. There is no one else exactly like you. Christian self-esteem consists of the ability to accept and celebrate the gifts, skills, and interests God has placed within you. This may be precisely the time in your life to discover what you can now do to more fully line up your abilities with what God has in mind for you.

God created us with three basic desires: the desire to belong, the desire to accomplish or achieve something, and the desire to be empowered to do what he wants us to do. In many ways, we partially meet these longings in a healthy marriage—through our intimacy, our mutual goals and interests, and empowering and encouraging one another. However, ultimately these are met in our relationship with Christ. We belong to him. He gives us the gifts and empowers us through his Spirit to be able to live and work for him by being a blessing to others as well as ourselves. The next time you look at yourself in the mirror, remind yourself that you are a treasure in God's eyes. Hopefully you are gradually feeling better about yourself even while going through the challenging changes from "we" to "me."

2

potholes and craters

Filling the Voids When No Longer Married

Gary's Journal: I used to dream I was lost and couldn't find my way back home. I believed my wife was waiting for me, but every time I turned a corner, I seemed to get farther and farther away. Last night the dream changed. She was the one who left. She was the one who didn't come back. I don't know where she went, but I woke up feeling disturbed in realizing she would never sleep with me again. We'd never make love again. I'd never feel her quiet breath on my cheek as we fell asleep at night. I am all alone. It seems like nothing will ever be able to fill the mammoth hole that her death left in my life. I really feel lost and overwhelmed with all she used to do that is now on me. How can I possibly manage two people's jobs and responsibilities around here?

Stacey's Journal: Part of this I really like. Tom's out of my life now, and I don't have to put up with his lies and deception. The angry voices have quieted, and the house is at peace. What a relief! But I wasn't prepared for doing this parenting business on my own. Now it's just me, Mandy, and Matt. Mandy needs braces, and Matt is trying out for football. Money. I'm working as hard as I can, but there doesn't seem to be enough to cover expenses since Tom left. The responsibility of managing the entire household by myself is pretty overwhelming. I hardly have any time for myself. I heard that I have to rediscover who I am, but how can I find the time when there is no one else around to help service the cars, mow the lawn, shuttle to practices, and supervise homework? How are the holes ever going to get filled? I'm only one person!

Are My Friends and Relatives Going to Be There for Me?

You are forced to face all kinds of changes as a single person, and you don't know who will be there to help you. How do you now manage your children (dependent and/or adult), friends and relatives, your living arrangements, finance and work issues, not to mention the lack of physical and emotional intimacy that you may have had with your spouse? Who is going to be supportive on your journey back to wholeness?

Accepting the reality that you are now single is something that no one else can do for you. You need to do that by and for yourself. That is something you ultimately have to decide to accept. At some level there is the realization that you alone are responsible for your life and the lives of your kids (if that is your situation). However, finding people who can be supportive, people who really care about you as you deal with all the new circumstances you are facing, is certainly helpful. They may be your adult children, parents, siblings, or close friends. Probably not everyone you thought would be there for you is there. But other people you never expected might have stepped up to the plate to encourage you. Most everyone who has gone through grief following the death or divorce of a spouse testifies that most of their relationships changed over the first couple of years after their marriage ended. Some of these relationships faded away; others became stronger. That may trouble you, but if you are at all typical, most of your friends were friends that you and your spouse had together. They have their own thoughts and feelings about what has happened, and they are trying to adapt to the empty place your spouse left in their lives as well. They may not know what to do for or with you now. You probably appear different to them because you are no longer partnered. You may feel hurt if they distance themselves from you. Hopefully you have a number of friends and family who are ready to stick with you through whatever you will have to face. While they can't rebuild your life for you, they certainly can support you in a wide variety of ways.

Even in what you may consider to be supportive relationships, a number of changes may occur. Your former in-laws may initially be involved in your life, but as time goes on you may notice a growing distance in that relationship either from your side or theirs. You may be hurt by this if you wanted to stay close. Actually, with a spousal death or a divorce, your previous spouse's parents are no longer legally your in-laws, since the marriage has officially come to an end. That doesn't mean you can't continue to have a relationship with them, but making the relationship work usually requires more effort on both sides. If you liked your in-laws while you were married, you may want to maintain a connection with them. On the other hand, if you didn't appreciate them very much (or they, you), the relationship will likely either end abruptly or gradually fade over time. You need to determine what kind of relationship you want to have with your previous spouse's side of the family, and from there consider options based on how their wishes fit with your desire for a continuing relationship. However, your dependent children still need your help and support in having contact with their grandparents on both sides of the family. The death or divorce of a parent is a profound change, and maintaining your children's relationships with both sides of the family will be immensely beneficial. When your children are adults, they will then be responsible for their own relationships with both sides of the family.

Your relationship with your children needs to be a priority as you carve out your new social network. Obviously if you have dependent children at home, your journey from "we" to "me" has to accommodate your responsibilities to your children. Typically children and young people will wait to grieve fully until their surviving or divorced parent has worked through much of his or her own personal grief and made healthy adjustments. Subconsciously, they don't want to risk placing further stress or demands on their surviving parent who may be struggling on the grief journey.

Words for the Widowed

You are no longer coupled, so many things your spouse did are no longer being taken care of. This is especially true with parenting your children. If your children are adults, they still need a close connection with you, and all the more because of the death of their other parent. If you are raising younger dependent children, you face a myriad of challenges. You no longer have a partner with whom to discuss the rules, infractions, and consequences for misbehavior or share encouraging words and praise when a child does something well. You have to make all the decisions by yourself. What curfew should you set for your teenagers? How many extracurricular activities can your middle-schooler be involved with? How do you handle parent-teacher conferences, especially when academic performance may be slipping? If your parents, your former in-laws, or other family and friends are available, their support can be helpful, but in no way can they replace an intact parenting team. Remember, you cannot do it all by yourself. Talk with your children about which of their activities they want to continue. Help them make realistic choices, and then find people who can help you assist them in maintaining some of their previous involvements.

Words for the Divorced

If you still have children at home, your new arrangement for parenting may seem strange and uncomfortable. Depending on the court's decision about custody and visitation rights, one of you will likely have primary responsibility as custodial parent. Even if you decided on a 50-50 split with joint custody of the children, you face a unique challenge to your parenting style. Typically you and your ex-spouse will be more physically and emotionally disconnected than ever before. Making joint decisions may be difficult unless you are fortunate enough to be in that minority of divorced couples who have parted amicably and work at maintaining consistency regarding expectations and consequences for their children. If you and your ex-spouse are both committed to providing quality parent-child experiences, the times your children are with their other parent may offer you a helpful physical and emotional break from child care without undue concern for their welfare.

Depending on the nature of your divorce, some of your family members and those of your former spouse may be unhappy with you. They may be angry or embarrassed that your marriage failed. They may not be very willing to help or support you. This may be especially true if they see you as the "responsible party" who caused or filed for the divorce. Family members usually support their blood relative, and friends tend to take sides (at least after a while), so usually no one in a divorce situation continues to experience the same level of support they may have had before the divorce was finalized. Having support withdrawn can hurt a great deal. Talk with them about what would be helpful for you. You will likely need to initiate these conversations. The more civil those relationships can be on both sides of the family and also with family friends, the better it will be for your children. That is especially true for younger children who are still at home. Once your children are established as adults, they can take the responsibility for their own decisions about how they wish to relate to both sides of their biological family.

45

What about My Home, Work, and Finances?

Now that you are single again, you face the challenge of maintaining your home, securing or continuing suitable employment, and achieving an adequate level of financial security. We empathize with you that these issues can consume a great deal of your emotional and physical energy as you move from "we" to "me."

Let's first of all talk about your home. Whether you own (or are buying) your home, rent an apartment, or have some other living arrangement, the healthiest approach is not to make any major changes to your housing situation within the first year after the death or divorce of a spouse if at all possible. Obviously, in the case of a divorce, one of you will have to find another place to live. Hopefully the custodial parent (if younger children are involved) will remain in the house at least during the divorce process itself. Finding more affordable housing may be necessary if you can't generate the income to support your current residence along with living expenses. However, consistency in keeping the environment as stable as possible for both you and your children is extremely important.

Perhaps you were a stay-at-home parent and did not work outside the home. Or maybe you had a part-time job to give you diversity, but it didn't add much to your household's financial support. If so, your finances may now be inadequate, and you need to find a different job to increase your income and provide benefits for you (and your children, if you have them). The process of finding a job and maintaining both a work and home schedule can feel overwhelming. Look for creative ways to prioritize aspects of home life that are the most significant for you, and try to delegate the remainder to supportive people in your life if they are available—at least in your adjustment phase.

You may also face a number of financial pressures. Perhaps you can't pay your rent or mortgage. You may have gone from a two-person to a one-person income. If your spouse died you may have some money available from a life insurance policy, and in the case of divorce, possibly alimony. In addition, you will receive Social Security payments for dependent children if widowed and child support if divorced. But you now have the entire financial responsibility to deal with by yourself. You may also have added debts because of medical, funeral, or attorney costs. We strongly recommend you see a financial advisor for an objective opinion about your options before making financial decisions.

People with adequate financial means, a stable job they like, and a home that is comfortable and affordable are in a better position to manage the death or a divorce of a spouse. The lack of any of these things produces more distress by distracting you from the grieving and rebuilding process because you must also cope with all the changes in your financial and living arrangements.

Change is difficult for most people, but kids are the least in control. They need to know if your financial resources have decreased and you need to find more affordable housing. Explain this to your children so they can understand why this is necessary *before* it happens. Decreased funds will also affect their choices for activities and expenditures. If presented in a realistic manner, most kids can adjust to these changes fairly well. Love, affection, discipline, and security don't cost anything, yet they are priceless. They are the crux of creating psychologically healthy and happy children.

Words for the Widowed

Depending on your age, you may not be financially secure after the death of your spouse. If you are young, your spouse may not have had adequate life insurance to pay off the mortgage or other major debts or have adequate investments to sustain you. So if you aren't already working outside the home, you may have to look for a job or get additional training to acquire employable skills. You may even have to sell your home. These financial pressures complicate an already extremely difficult and stressful situation. Obviously the more you are forced to work outside the home for financial reasons, the greater your challenge in finding the time to do necessary grief work.

On the other hand, some people who have been widowed face quite a different financial situation. Perhaps your spouse had a huge life insurance policy or other investments that suddenly catapult you into a higher financial tier than to what you were accustomed. You may feel guilty being financially benefitted through your spouse's death. Be careful to seek solid, reliable financial advice before you are emotionally tempted to make generous charitable donations or give large sums of money to your children. Grief can obscure your ability to think straight, and waiting at least a year, if not two or three if you can, to make major financial decisions is good advice.

If you are retired or close to it, you may be more financially stable because of your advanced planning. However, you still need to be wise about how you manage your income from investments, your own Social Security benefits (and if you both worked, you are now receiving only one of the two checks), and/or any other pensions because you are living on a "fixed" income.

Words for the Divorced

The adage "two can live cheaper than one" likely rings true as you try to forge ahead on your own. As a couple you may have been able to manage financially quite well, but now you and your ex-spouse will each have to set up separate households, and you have sole financial responsibility for one of them. If you have physical custody of dependent children, you will most likely receive child support payments and possibly alimony if you were married long enough. That will help for the period of time designated in your divorce agreement. At the time of the divorce proceedings, we hope you advocated for a fair and equitable financial settlement because this will be the launching pad for your financial future. A huge disparity in the levels of income between you and your ex-spouse may be disconcerting to the one who has the lower income. Along with that, the one having more resources may be tempted to buy the children's affections through gifts and special events. The other parent may initially fear looking like Scrooge to younger children, and then appearing to not love them as much. Just remember that teaching kids the value of working for things they want and experiencing some delayed gratification will serve them better throughout their life.

As the divorce is being finalized, the family home will often be sold for financial reasons, and each of you will need to make your own living arrangements. Dependent children will experience more stability by having their own space in each of your households. If incomes are high enough and you are the custodial parent, you may be able to remain in the family home until the youngest child graduates from high school and reaches the age of eighteen. Then you can institute an equitable procedure in keeping with your divorce settlement to divide the earnings from the sale of the home between you and your ex-spouse.

Who Will Hug Me Now? Dealing with Touch and Intimacy Issues

Physical touch is extremely important to all of us. We long to be touched or hugged appropriately by our family and friends. In a marriage relationship, we expect to have an intimate physical relationship including caressing and mutual lovemaking. When this physical touch is absent, we often experience "skin hunger," a normal physical and emotional response to the lack of touch and closeness. Because your marriage has ended, you may be asking yourself, "How will I ever get my physical needs met now that I am single?" The loss of physical intimacy is significant in itself, and now that you have been widowed or divorced, you face a moral and practical challenge to find a way to manage this skin hunger and your sexuality. As a single person you need to decide if you will practice sexual abstinence, use some form of self-pleasuring, or have some level of a physical relationship with another partner. Your challenge is to construct boundaries consistent with your values and beliefs.

There are ways to help satisfy skin hunger that don't conflict with or challenge a person's value system. Hugging yourself, applying lotion to your body and enjoying a refreshing shower or bubble bath are some ways to experience physical touch that may give you some sensory satisfaction. Various forms of exercise may also be of benefit, such as swimming, walking vigorously, jogging, doing yard work, or participating in some sport. You might also ask for hugs from your family or friends, get a massage, schedule a manicure or pedicure, go someplace to dance, or select a purposeful cause to displace some pent-up physical energy. While engaging in activities that provide some physical and/or sexual release of energy, be aware of the physical skin sensations they produce to determine which activities are most helpful to meet your individual needs.

Of course, there is no getting around the fact that none of these methods will fully measure up to the kind of physical touch and intimacy you may have had in a reasonably good marriage. Acknowledging this significant change in your life is an extremely important step in coming to grips with the reality of being single. Your challenge is to find creative ways to either express and/or sublimate your physical and sexual needs in ways that maintain your integrity.

Words for the Widowed

If you had a sexually fulfilling marriage, you undoubtedly experience a huge hole in the place of your physical relationship. Hopefully you have warm memories of the joy physical intimacy brought to your life. For many widowed persons, sexual needs are repressed during the early days or months of grieving because the pain of loss is so profound. Gradually, however, most people become increasingly aware of missing the physical closeness they had with their partner. Journaling about this void helps most people to some extent. You now face the challenge of dealing with your skin hunger and sexual needs on a long-term basis in the ways mentioned above or through some other creative outlet.

Words for the Divorced

Divorce implies that the marriage was likely strained and intimacy between the partners probably had waned some time back. Physical and emotional closeness were likely shattered by anger and resentment. At least one of you in the relationship may have felt rejected, victimized, or ignored and therefore was probably uninterested in a physical relationship or experienced a decrease in sexual fulfillment. However, we want to reaffirm that we are all sexual beings and that some form of physical touch and affirmation is important to a sense of self-esteem and internal well-being. As you work through your loss, your challenge will be to find ways to become whole again physically and sexually that feel congruent for you.

my spiritual journey across the potholes and craters

If you were widowed, what did the vow "till death do us part" really mean?

"Till death do us part"—this phrase is professed in wedding ceremonies almost as frequently as the "Star Spangled Banner" is sung at sporting events. Rarely do people actually focus on the deeper meaning of the words. They don't want to think or talk about death at a wedding! Many of us who have been widowed claim that we never expected it to happen. The words "till death do us part" never really registered.

Or we subconsciously added: ". . . when we are very old and hopefully die together."

So now maybe you turn to the Bible to give you the confidence that someday you will be reunited with your spouse and that your marital love will rekindle in eternity. But sadly, the Bible never gives that message. On the contrary, Jesus actually said that we will neither marry nor be given in marriage in heaven. How can God give us such a wonderful experience called marriage and not keep it going in heaven? The Bible really asks us to think outside the box when it comes to our relationships in eternity. On earth, marriage is a legal decree, and we are related to others by bloodline. In heaven, all relationships are established through the blood of Jesus Christ. We will all gather around his throne as sisters and brothers in Christ. We believe we will know each other. We may even have our same names! But you will not experience your husband or wife as your spouse but rather as a brother or sister in Christ. What is even more amazing is that even the best marriage relationship a couple might have on this earth will pale in contrast to the beauty and intimacy to be experienced in the new relationships we will have within the eternal family of God.

What does the Bible say about remarriage if I was widowed or divorced?

The Bible is very clear that a widowed person is free to remarry if he or she desires. The situation for someone who was divorced appears to be more complicated than for someone who was widowed. Jesus taught that divorce was allowed only in case of adultery. For many who read these words, this may sound like bad news. Many marriages fail for reasons other than blatant sexual violation of the marriage contract. Irreconcilable differences, addictive behaviors, a lack of intimacy, abuse, or growing distance between the partners are all frequent reasons why marriages fail.

But look at the rest of the story. The gospel means "good news," and what is the "good news" here? Quite simply: God forgives. Divorce is not an unforgivable sin. As a matter of fact, according to the Bible we are all sinners, every day and in every way. If you truly understand the Bible, the question never was "Am I a sinner?" Of course, we all are! The Bible says that all of us, whether we were divorced or not, were dead in sin and deserving of God's judgment.

So you can be forgiven for the divorce, but does that also mean you are free to remarry? Some church traditions would have you think that if you remarry after an "unbiblical" divorce you are committing "continuous adultery." We believe, however, that this does not fully honor the nature of God's forgiveness. If you truly repent of whatever you might have done to contribute to your divorce, and if you have fully accepted Christ's forgiveness, we believe that forgiveness has wiped away that past error. At that point, you are "right" with God and in his eyes you are free to remarry according to the Protestant faith. Catholics first need to go through the annulment process, but then they are free to remarry.

The following principles summarize the Bible's teaching about a divorce on grounds other than adultery and a subsequent remarriage.

First: divorce is a sin, but realize that we are all sinners.

Second: no single sin is greater or worse than any other. Jesus taught that even thinking sinful thoughts (which we all do) is just as bad as actually committing the sin.

Third: God's forgiveness comes freely, just for the asking. All you need to do is confess your sin, and God totally forgives and removes it from you. He wipes the slate clean, and you are free to begin again—even to remarry in a God-fearing way.

Fourth: God's forgiveness does come with an obligation. The challenge is now to grow from the experience. That is why in many cases Christians who truly grow through the experience of divorce can, with God's blessing, enter into a more satisfying life. Whether you choose to remain single or decide to remarry, perhaps your biggest challenge will be learning how to forgive yourself and how to rebuild your life in a way that honors your Christian faith.

How can I be confident that God will provide for my financial and material needs?

Frequently following a death or divorce, you face major changes in finances and material possessions. While sometimes a large life insurance payment or a generous court judgment may increase your financial stability, more frequently the loss of a second income (if your spouse was working) and many of the other costs of living on your own raise your anxiety. We all know the Bible tells us not to worry—to have faith. But the bills still come each month, and the balance in the checkbook can't meet the needs. Let's do two things for a moment. First, let's dig a little deeper into this issue of the relationship between finances and our faith in God. Then let's consider a strategy to use during this time of financial transition that honors God *and* may give you a little more peace of mind during some tough times.

You may be familiar with Jesus's parable about the talents in Matthew. If not, you can read about it in Matthew 25:14–30. This story contains four principles that may help you understand the relationship between our possessions and our faith. The first principle is that *everything belongs to God.* The master owned all the bags of gold. They were his possessions, and when he returned he expected to be given an account of how *his* investments had fared.

Second, *God entrusted this gift to us.* Everything we have is a gift from God. We are to care for it, nurture it, invest it, but ultimately it still belongs to God. The master gave his servants various sums of money and gave them the prerogative to do whatever they judged appropriate with the money. He entrusted this gift to them.

Third, he not only entrusts these gifts to us, but *he gives them to us for our enjoyment.* The one who buried it in the ground was motivated by fear. For those servants who actually invested the money, they likely experienced the joy of the growth of their investment. All the gifts we receive from God are blessings that he generously gives to us.

Fourth, *everything God entrusts to us is to be used for his kingdom.* The master returned at the end of the story and expected both the original gift as well as the growth to be returned to him. All that God gives us ultimately returns to his kingdom.

So what does this mean for you as you try to find your way through a major financial transition? Understand that you (and your spouse) never really owned anything. It all belongs to God. Even if you practiced tithing (giving 10 percent back to God through a church or another charitable organization), God still owns the other 90 percent as well.

Believe the Bible when God says he will take care of you. He tells us to seek his kingdom first, confident that he will take care of everything else. But also understand that God's timing can be very different from yours.

Simplify. You may not need all the things you have accumulated. You may not need to engage in all the leisure activities or travels you did when married. Take a hard look at your lifestyle to decide what you really need. You may wish to read a book such as Richard Foster's *Freedom of Simplicity*[2] to help you think through these lifestyle decisions.

Finally, be wise and discerning. Like the faithful servants in the parable of the talents, God also expects you to make wise decisions about your financial matters. So do your part by using the open doors he provides to help yourself become more financially secure.

3

deciding to remain "me" or become "we" again

Singleness versus Dating

Amanda's Journal: For a long time after my husband died, the thought of being intimate with another man was simply nauseating. We had a good sex life. How could I ever do that with someone else? But I am beginning to miss the companionship and the physical intimacy. A lot of people are encouraging me to get into another relationship, but honestly, I kind of like being in control of my own life, not having to compromise with someone else. I also like my freedom—the flexibility that I have. But I miss . . . Oh, my! This is so tough!

Josh's Journal: Talk about being in a difficult place! I'm still shell-shocked by the divorce even though it happened over a year ago. The marriage ended, but my ex-spouse and I still have a connection through the kids, though a much different one. I realize that I miss an intimate relationship and am starting to notice other women in a way I hadn't before. I think I could initiate something—a date, a relationship, who knows—maybe even eventually another marriage. But I don't think I'm ready for that yet. I'm not sure I'm over my ex in all the ways I need to be. I probably have to figure things out on my own for a while longer before I try dating.

Will I or Won't I?

By the time you get to the point of asking yourself, "Will I choose to remain single, or do I want to date and possibly remarry?" you have already made many major decisions. You likely remember when you could barely get out of bed, not wanting to face the day. Now you may wonder what the rest of your life will look like, and whether or not you want to share your life with someone new. If you ask that question too early in your journey from "we" to "me," you may run headlong into a number of problems. For one thing, you really have to be through the grieving process to make the best decision for you. Also realize that the divorce rate for second marriages is higher than for first, and that rate is even higher if you make the decision to marry before the end of the first year of grieving your loss. There are both advantages and disadvantages in remaining single, dating, or remarrying, so know your own thoughts and feelings about these options to choose wisely.

Words for the Widowed

Early in grief, most widowed people react quite negatively when someone asks if they are ready to date. Words such as *nauseating* and *repulsive* are frequently used to describe their reaction. You may have been so fraught with the devastation of your loss that you were afraid to even contemplate letting someone else get close again and chance repeating that intense hurt. And the idea that you could ever be emotionally and physically close to another person probably seemed unbelievable. You may still feel a sense of loyalty to your deceased spouse if your marriage was happy. Getting involved with someone else may seem to you (and perhaps, you fear, to others) like you really didn't love your spouse. Of course, in reality, you can't be disloyal to someone who is no longer here or available. On the other hand, perhaps you were unhappy in your marriage or your partner was ill for a long time so you now feel relieved that you can do things you want, including to date.

Men often approach dating differently than women because of how they experience their spouse's death. They tend to feel that they have "lost" a part of themselves or have been dismembered, so their normal inclination is to "fix" this situation quickly by trying to replace what they lost. These replacement relationships present any number of problems and rarely survive long term. Women, on the other hand, typically feel abandoned or deserted by their partner, and therefore take much longer to work through their sense of being left behind. So they usually do not venture into dating nearly as soon as men do.

Will I or won't I? You can't answer that question in a healthy way until you have traveled the entire grief journey, which lasts, at the very least, one year, have redefined your own personal life, embraced and accepted the fact that you are single, and can really attest to the advantages of being on your own. Only then can you decide if you want to date and perhaps move into another relationship.

Words for the Divorced

Your sense of failure and hurt may have left you leery about dating or marrying again. Once was enough. Being minimized, ignored, devalued, and sometimes taken advantage of took their toll. Fear of repeating the same mistakes and ending up divorced again may haunt you. You might feel that you aren't "marriage material" since your previous marriage didn't last. What caused the breakdown in your marriage? What was lacking that the two of you couldn't rebuild? How did you contribute to the end of your former marriage? Make a list of dating pros and cons based on what you've learned about yourself, your previous marriage(s), and your future goals and life's purposes. Making this list will help you answer these important questions. Thinking positively about yourself and identifying what you have to offer a coupled relationship are necessary precursors to deciding to remain single or begin dating.

The Choice of Remaining Single

You may decide to remain single. Dating or remarriage may not appeal to you for a variety of reasons. If you have evaluated your options and honestly chosen to remain single for its own merits, then don't be swayed by the opinions of others. Trust that you know what is best for you. Some people think that being single is inferior to marriage or is only a temporary holding pattern until you meet someone special. However, deciding to stay single can be a healthy choice. But don't choose to remain single as a way to avoid working through the issues that arose in your prior marriage. You need to resolve those issues and address all the accompanying emotions regardless of which option you choose.

In today's culture, being a single adult is much more acceptable than it was a few decades ago. Many people decide they don't want to risk a new relationship that has more than a 50-50 chance of ending in divorce. As people age, they bring more and more baggage with them from the past and have already developed their own ingrained pattern of living. So trying to accommodate to another person may not sound good to you. You may have dependent children at home and decide that raising them as a single parent would be best for them and less complicated for you. Stepparenting and introducing stepsiblings into the home can be difficult and stressful, especially when it involves adolescents who are already pushing against family rules as they begin to emancipate. The decision to remain single is by no means an inferior one, nor does it suggest you are a failure. If occasionally you want to connect with someone of the opposite sex, you can date simply to enjoy meeting new people and to engage in a variety of activities without making another lifelong commitment. Developing opposite-sex friendships, in addition to those of your same gender, is a way to satisfy your social needs without involvement in a more intimate relationship.

The Pros and Cons of Remaining Single

We have listed some of the pros and cons of remaining single. See if these resonate with you and add any other positive or negative factors that are specific to your life situation.

Pros of Remaining Single

1. You can make your own decisions without considering or compromising with someone else (such as, how to spend your time, utilize financial resources, develop friendships, etc.).
2. You can take better care of yourself because you can focus on your own needs without being distracted by someone else's.
3. You can do whatever you want when you want to in pursuing your own interests.
4. You can develop close personal relationships, as you want to, with people of the opposite sex.
5. You don't run the risk of being widowed or divorced again.
6. You don't have to deal with stepfamily issues or someone else's ex-spouse.
7. You have no partner to whom you need to be accountable.

Cons of Remaining Single

1. If you have children, you have sole responsibility for them as minors and for keeping a healthy relationship with your adult children and their families.

2. You no longer have an intimate physical, emotional, and spiritual relationship with a spouse with whom you plan daily events or make longer-term decisions.
3. You lack intimate sexual expression when your moral code limits it exclusively to marriage.
4. You no longer have a partner who shares financial obligations and responsibilities.
5. You need to find your own support and care when you are ill.
6. You have the sole responsibility for all your daily tasks of living, such as household tasks and maintenance, care of your vehicle, etc.
7. You may be lonely more of the time.

Words for the Widowed

As your grief subsides and you sense a new person emerging within you, phrases like "I still like this!" or "I can do this!" become more prominent in your thoughts. Your life can actually become exciting again! Many people who have been widowed begin to feel invigorated and empowered as they rebuild their lives. They discover a new freedom and independence. They can go to a movie whenever they want, go golfing on a whim, or visit some distant relatives or friends on the spur of the moment.

There are a number of reasons why widowed people may not want to date or remarry. You may have come through a long period of caring for your ailing spouse prior to his or her death and are now relieved of that heavy responsibility. When you contemplate dating, you may be afraid you will have to repeat that caregiving role should your new partner become ill.

Even if you want to date and possibly remarry, women are at a distinct disadvantage since the ratio of single women to men is approximately four to one by the time you are at midlife or beyond. If you are a female and only want to date a person who has been widowed, finding someone can be especially challenging. Whether you are a man or a woman, we certainly encourage you to learn to live on your own, learn to love yourself, become empowered by your own skills and talents, and then decide if you prefer to be in a close, intimate relationship once again. The decision to remain single is a perfectly healthy one, and a high percentage of widowed persons purposely choose this option. They are not "left behind." They decided to move from a "we" to a "me" and remain single, enjoying a full, rich, and satisfying life for themselves.

Words for the Divorced

Having gone through a divorce, you may be gun-shy, thinking you might wind up divorced again. You may want to play it safe. But remaining single to avoid that fear is not a healthy reason. Even those who were in a conflictual, unhappy marriage often want to find a fulfilling and satisfying one in the future. The most important thing you need to do before deciding to date and remarry is to evaluate what you contributed both positively and negatively to your former marriage. Once you evaluate what you did well and how you contributed to the breakup in your past marriage, you can rework problematic attitudes and behaviors before you enter into another relationship. Moving through this process, you might even discover that remaining single could be a more satisfying and fulfilling option than getting married again.

He/She Is Just a Friend! The Rewards and Consequences of Heterosexual Friendships

We all need people in our lives, even though some of us may want more social connections than others based on our unique personalities, needs, and desires. When your marriage ended either by death or divorce, all of your relationships experienced a major shift. No matter how many friendships you currently have, you will want to make some new ones with people who know you only as a single person. Developing friendships specifically with people who have experienced a loss similar to yours provides a common bond where both of you can legitimately say "I have some idea of what you're going through and how your life is changing." You can share your stories of loss, talk about how you are coping with these life-altering changes, and more effectively encourage each other.

Developing friendships with both men and women is extremely beneficial for single adults. Both of the genders often relate differently because of environmental and societal influences. Although talking with a person of your same sex can be helpful, comforting, and encouraging, talking with someone of the opposite sex may provide a perspective you might not get from your own gender. But remember that while still grieving, you are vulnerable, especially to a person of the opposite sex who may show interest in you. Being alone with that person may elicit unexpected physical and emotional reactions and reduce your ability to think clearly. For that reason, we recommend you not meet on a one-to-one basis with someone of the opposite sex until you decide you are ready and want to date. Before that time comes, limit your contacts with the opposite sex to group gatherings, which provide a safer emotional and physical environment.

Deciding to Take the Plunge: Learning to Date in a Different World

You are ready to date when you have dealt with and resolved issues related to your loss and are no longer in emotional pain. If you then decide to date, realize that dating can have two quite different objectives and essentially take two different pathways. First, you can date to develop friendships with the opposite sex, expand your world, and in the process learn more about yourself. Second, you can date to find someone with whom you might want to have a serious relationship and possibly marry. Let's take a minute to expand on both perspectives.

We already suggested that developing healthy opposite-sex friendships is one way to fill some of the void created by the loss of your spouse. Dating can provide companionship and fun through sharing mutually enjoyable activities. You aren't limited to the interests you would pursue alone or with friends of your own gender. Many people date a variety of people with no intention of establishing a long-term committed relationship. If that is your choice, make certain the person you are dating knows you aren't looking for a relationship that would progress to a more serious level.

The second reason to date is to find someone you want to marry. In this case you search for someone who meets your criteria for a mate and date him or her to see if the two of you are compatible for marriage.

You can get hurt emotionally if your reasons for dating aren't clear to both you and the person you are dating. You may feel uncomfortable talking about what each of your purposes for dating are, especially early in the relationship. However, if you don't clarify that relatively soon and the two of you are looking for different things from the relationship, one of you could become emotionally attached and therefore hurt when the relationship doesn't move to a more serious level. As much as possible, avoid becoming involved with a person who does not have the same goal for dating as you do. Healthy dating consists of two people who have similar ideas about where they hope the dating experience will lead. Even if the two of you are in sync with your reason for dating, don't presume the relationship will work out. One of the purposes of dating is to explore your compatibility. You may decide after a few dates not to see this person again because he or she isn't compatible with your list of criteria.

No matter which perspective you are coming from, we urge you to write down the characteristics you would want in a potential future marriage partner. These include things such as personality and character traits, values and beliefs, lifestyle, interests, etc. List as well the things you would not want or won't tolerate in another person. Those may be age differences, age of children, addictive behaviors, financial or job instability, lack of or different religious beliefs, a strong opposing political preference, a legal history, and/or a serious disease or health issues. Remember, people usually don't change their life patterns for another person. If you conclude early on that a person does not meet your criteria for a future marriage partner, do each of you a favor and make that clear as soon as you realize it. You may have anxiety about putting your thoughts and feelings into words, but trust us, speaking up is very important for your future and for good self-care. You might say something like: "We aren't as compatible as I had hoped. From my perspective there are too many differences between us for me to want to continue dating. I did appreciate the opportunity to meet you, and I wish you the best."

Words for the Widowed

Once the pain of being widowed recedes because of the grief work you have done, you are likely more open to different experiences, and so finding someone new to spend time with may sound appealing. Many people think that if your previous marriage was a healthy one, you could never achieve that same level of emotional and physical intimacy again. But that is simply not true. Over time you can attach to another person and experience at least a similar, if not deeper, level of closeness than what you had before because of all you have learned about life in dealing with the loss of your spouse. Likewise, if your prior marriage was conflictual and unhealthy, you can develop a much closer, more intimate relationship than you had previously.

You may want to date only someone who, like you, has been widowed. Dating a person who has been divorced may be a "deal breaker" because you think that marrying a widowed person has a higher probability of success than marrying someone who was divorced. Dealing with the fact that a divorced person had a marriage that failed is often a major concern. You may not want to put up with the presence of an ex-spouse either. But don't fool yourself into thinking that a widowed person necessarily had a healthy marriage. Some widowed persons may have been in a dysfunctional marriage or on the brink of divorce before the death occurred. In any case, whether your prospective date was widowed, divorced, or never married, learn how he or she has grown from those experiences and what he or she still needs to address to be a healthy partner in a future marriage.

If you were in a happy marriage, you may be tempted to date someone who is similar to your deceased spouse. But be aware of two things. First, obviously no one will fit his or her mold, and if you try to replicate your previous marriage you may be tempted to make a lot of comparisons. Second, in attempting to find someone like your previous partner, you may forego an opportunity to have a totally different and possibly more exciting partner in the next phase of your life. Venture into new arenas and date a variety of people who meet your criteria.

Words for the Divorced

Your previous marriage didn't work out as you hoped and dreamed. Perhaps you may not have had a choice in the matter because your spouse was the one who wanted it to end. You may now feel a little shaky about trying to date again. Maybe you think you will be seen as having "failed." Others may wonder why you couldn't hold your marriage together. But remember, one person can't make a marriage healthy. Remind yourself of what you have learned to do differently to make your next marriage successful. If you are going to date to possibly find another marriage partner, remember you have as much right to a happy marriage as anyone else. But be aware of the rebound effect. Don't be dazzled only by what the other person has that your previous partner didn't. Consider the whole picture. Keep assessing the person even after he or she begins to look good to you to avoid any blind spots that could come back to haunt you.

The Three *P*s Regarding Dating

Deciding to date without any forethought as to your safety and well-being is extremely unwise. Therefore, consider three *P*s as you begin dating—the Precautions, Protocols, and Possibilities.

Here Are Some PRECAUTIONS to Keep in Mind

- *Be careful how you go about finding someone to date.* We think it best to meet someone through a mutual acquaintance if at all possible. If you are using an internet dating site, be aware that people can present themselves any way they want to, and you have no good way to prove or disprove a person's credibility (such as if the person is actually single) until you spend time together. If you are going to attempt to meet someone online, check out the website(s) carefully. Find out what kind of background checks they do on people who post their entries with them. How are the matches made—by a computer, a person, or simply self-selected by members themselves? Some dating websites charge a membership fee (and some have other hidden costs), but there are a number of free websites that may be worth checking out first. When you finally meet a person, move slowly and have frequent face-to-face contact in a variety of settings to learn who this person really is.
- *Be safe when meeting a new person for the first time.* Giving someone you are going to date information about

where you live, particularly if you have no references for the person, is very risky. Meet him or her several times in a public place and drive separately so you can leave when you want. Only after you have enough data about the person's mental and emotional health and are confident this person is safe and trustworthy should you give out your address and drive places together. Another part of being safe is to keep your drink, purse, or wallet with you at all times.

- *Know the goal of dating for yourself and the person you are dating.* Make certain that you have similar goals of what you want out of dating. As we said earlier, you can be hurt, frustrated, or waste your time if you are dating to find someone you might want to marry but the other person doesn't want that. You may be afraid to ask about his or her purpose for dating because you fear rejection, you might get hurt, and it may end the relationship. But in the long run, breaking off a relationship after you have already developed a significant emotional and physical attachment is much more painful than doing it earlier in the relationship.

- *Set your own physical and sexual boundaries for a dating relationship before you begin to date.* If you have been without your previous spouse for a period of time and enjoyed physical closeness in that marriage, you will likely be vulnerable to a date's touch, even as little as a touch on the arm or a brief kiss. Define the boundaries of what you would do physically with another person incrementally (after what length of time) and where you want to stop until marriage. This may be a hug after two or three dates and then progressing to light kissing with no other physical expression until the relationship develops further. Someone who values a relationship with you will respect and honor your boundaries while continuing to date you. If that is not the case, that person may be more interested in a sexual relationship rather than first developing emo-

69

tional intimacy with you. Forming emotional closeness is necessary to provide a sturdy foundation for a committed relationship.

- *Keep your head intact when dating a person rather than letting your feelings get ahead of you.* A significant area to pay attention to in dating is being objective about deciding who to date. You may be tempted to say, "I just want to give him or her a chance." But if the relationship doesn't seem practical, logical, or a good idea at the beginning, it won't in the end either. One significant factor, from our perspective, is that the person you date must have at least one year after a divorce or the death of a spouse under his or her belt before you date that person. Don't fall into the trap of wanting a relationship so badly that you throw out your healthy reasoning ability. Everyone has some good qualities, but the entire package of the person you are dating has to be considered carefully before you make a decision to continue to date. By all means, don't let a physical connection develop before you are convinced that this person is a good choice for you to date. Being physical at any level can obstruct objective thinking and a balanced evaluation of a person. If new concerns about the person emerge later on, evaluate those to see if they are significant enough to end the relationship. Don't tolerate unhealthy behavior or fool yourself into believing you can change the person. What you see early on is generally what you get long term as well.

- *Be wise about how you will involve your children.* We recommend you wait until your dating relationship has become serious enough that you would consider marrying this person before introducing him or her to your children. Your kids don't need to meet everyone in your life. They may become confused or disillusioned with a variety of people coming in and out of their lives. That doesn't mean that dating should be kept a secret. Your children need to know when you are ready to date and that you are through dealing with the loss of your previous partner. Obviously, as you go out, you should let them know you are going on a date or are beginning to see a person more regularly. Reassure them that when you determine that the dating relationship has long-term potential, they will be able to meet the person.

Here Are Some PROTOCOLS to Keep in Mind

- *Decide whether or not to initiate a date.* A few decades ago, the man was usually the one who asked the woman out and paid for the date. Thankfully, either gender can now initiate a date. And who pays is also up for grabs. Usually the initiator pays, or the expense is split evenly. If you continue to date the same person, you should discuss openly who covers the cost of the date. Sometimes the decision of who pays is based on who makes more money and can afford it, but make certain you are wise about not investing a great deal more financially in the relationship than the other person does. Especially if your incomes are somewhat similar, try to keep your own financial contributions toward dating expenses equal.

- *Assess how decisions are made and watch for control issues.* A healthy dating relationship is like a legal scale with each side in balance with the other. That means that both persons need to participate equally when communicating. Assess your date's ability to express his or her thoughts and feelings openly, intently listen to what you have to say, and be able to compromise with you in making decisions, resolving differences, or settling conflicts. Be cautious about someone who exerts more power in making decisions without considering your input equally. Relationships don't work well, in our opinion, when your date exerts most of the control, leaving you to acquiesce to his or her wishes.

- *Keep conversations mutually balanced.* Occasionally we hear someone complaining that their date seemed uninterested in their life but was very willing to talk about his or hers. That communication style seems arrogant and narcissistic. In healthy conversations, each person is interested in their date's life, including thoughts and feelings about any topic that comes up in the course of the date. Be on guard if you are dating someone who asks very few questions or shows little interest in what you have to say.

- *Watch for "swallowing" thoughts and feelings.* You will want to work together to create an open, respectful environment in which you both can state what you think and feel. A truly healthy person recognizes that you are as important as he or she is and that what you have to say needs to be listened to and respected. Your dating partner may censor sharing some topics or issues because he or she is embarrassed or afraid that you might be critical or get angry. Withholding what you think or feel about anything is blatantly unhealthy for both you and your potential relationship. What is withheld gets stored inside, and the pile gets bigger the more that is done. These accumulated feelings may eventually explode in an angry outburst or some physical symptoms. Watch for this pattern in your date, but also know that if you are silent about an issue, your date can assume that whatever has been said is okay with you, because silence typically signifies agreement. Generally the underlying motivation for withholding an opinion is the sense that your opinion is not as valid or significant as that of your dating partner. Besides being untrue, withholding your viewpoint decreases your own sense of value and worth.

- *Keep the planning of activities balanced.* Whoever of the two of you initiates and plans activities needs to keep both your interests in mind. If one person dominates

72

the decision-making process of what you will do from one date to the next, that person is exercising too much control and the relationship will not deepen. This pattern may also demonstrate a lack of investment on the part of the person who withdraws from participating in the planning.

- *Watch for an unhealthy or stagnant relationship.* If, as you date, you decide that the relationship is unhealthy, have the courage and self-respect to end it. This may be difficult and painful at the time, but remaining in an unhealthy dating relationship compromises your future happiness. There are more "fish in the sea," even though you may not want to let go of this one right now. But holding on means you are stuck with an unhealthy situation that will affect your life long term.

Here Are Some POSSIBILITIES to Keep in Mind

- *Dating can open up the possibility of meeting new people and having different experiences.* Dating has the potential to add spark, excitement, and adventure to your life and offer new possibilities and directions through involvement in a wider variety of activities. Deciding to date, however, presents challenges and exposes you to some risk. You need to be careful in searching for someone to be involved with on a long-term basis.

- *Dating opens up the possibility of expanding your base of companionship and support.* With a broader social network, you increase the number of people who may be available to care for and support you as the need arises. But don't forget that dating can also offer an unexpected surprise at times. It is possible that even if you never intended to remarry, you may find someone who meets all of your criteria and changes your thinking, opening yourself up to the possibility of getting married again.

73

my spiritual journey in finding "me"

*Does God really prefer that I remain single after my
spouse died or I divorced?*

One of the biggest issues you face when rebuilding your
life after the death or divorce of your spouse is to decide
how you want to live the rest of your life. In this chapter we
have been addressing the question of whether or not you
want to remain single, possibly date, or even get married
again. Some churches espouse two beliefs based on what
they think the Bible implies: first, if your spouse died or
you are divorced, it is better for you to remain unmarried
for the rest of your life; and second, if you are divorced, you
will be committing continuous adultery if you remarry. If
these two beliefs were in fact what God wanted, your future
might look pretty bleak. Let's focus on the first belief here,
since we have already dealt with the issue of divorce and
remarriage in chapter 2.

The first thing to remember is that the early church experienced deep internal conflict and pressure from its pagan
culture. Sexual immorality was rampant in society, and in an
extreme reaction to that, some early Christians advocated
complete sexual celibacy. The church was torn in two over
the issue of sexuality and faith—especially because many
people were making rules rather than helping individuals
make responsible Christian decisions.

So when the apostle Paul entered the discussion, he gave
solid Christian advice—not just a list of rules. With respect to
the question of whether an unmarried person should remain
single or get married again, Paul's answer was driven by two
factors. He appealed, first of all, to basic biblical principles,
and second, to how a Christian can apply those principles to
their current situation. The biblical principle is that marriage
is designed not only to produce children but also to provide
a close personal relationship in this life. Paul even used mar-

riage as an analogy of the relationship between Christ and his church. But from his perspective, since he believed Christ was coming back very soon, he wanted believers to focus on Christ without being distracted by worldly relationships like marriage. As good as marriage may be, Paul was saying that if you could remain celibate (as he was) for the few years remaining before Christ's return, you could better concentrate on witnessing for the Lord in that pagan world. He did go on to say that if your sexual desire could not be easily contained, then marriage would still be a fine option, but that worldly concerns (including marriage) should not distract you from your Christian calling.

We live over two thousand years later, but we still live in a society where sexual promiscuity is prevalent. We also know that with every passing day, Christ's return is coming closer. But the Bible is really saying that while we wait, remember that God created marriage. If the opportunity arises for you to remarry, know there is nothing in the Bible that prohibits you. Actually, the decisions to remain single or remarry are both biblically legitimate options. The question is basically how you can best serve God while remaining sexually pure either by remaining single or deciding to date and remarry.

How do I let God lead in my decision-making? Will he give a sign to guide me?

Some people talk as though they have a direct pipeline to God when it comes to making decisions. They say things like "God told me to . . ." or "God led me to . . ." But perhaps you, like so many others, struggle to discern God's will for the many decisions you have to make as you work at rebuilding your life. Should I sell my home? Begin dating? Hire help for all the domestic responsibilities? Prior to the death or divorce of your spouse, ideally the two of you could consult on these matters and would come to some consensus on what you thought was the right thing to do.

Some years ago Christians were more inclined to use the phrase "the Lord willing" when they made plans for the future. You might not hear it said as frequently today, but the phrase is certainly biblical. What does it mean to say "the Lord willing"? Are you waiting to hear a voice from heaven? Are you looking for a specific sign or signal from God? Are you seeking a deep sense of conviction in your heart? To understand what the Bible has to say about this, we begin with the Lord's Prayer because that is basically the framework for conversation with God. The prayer teaches that there is a certain order of priority for how to go about praying. When you want to know God's will on something specific, you usually begin with a specific request: "Dear Lord, help me know if I should sell my house." But the Lord's Prayer suggests that some other things come *before* making such requests. The prayer begins with "Our Father who is in heaven, hallowed be your name," acknowledging that God and his majesty come before anything else in this entire world. Then the prayer adds, "Your kingdom come," to embrace the reality that God is totally in control of everything in this world. He is the King, and this entire universe is his kingdom. "Your will be done on earth as it is done in heaven," denotes that this matter of God's will is *not* tied to any specific need or request; it is presented as a state or condition of living. To pray this petition is to submit yourself to his authority and direction, somewhat like acknowledging that he is the pilot or driver in your life. He is in control, not you. You must trust that his will is good, gracious, perfect, and filled with purpose—a purpose that in the long run is best for you and your life.

You can be confident then that in many situations there may not be only one "God-willed" choice. If you are living within the will of God and seek his kingdom first, you may find that deciding for either option A or option B would honor the will of God. God's will, you see, is not necessarily something static associated with one specific situation or another. Living in God's will is simply living in a way that acknowledges that God is the Lord of your life. He expects you to make decisions as best you can. Often he blesses those decisions. Sometimes he redirects them. So you may make whatever plans you want, but you are encouraged to add "the Lord willing," for he is without question the one you need to direct your life.

What does the Bible say about dealing with sexuality as a single adult?

Now that you are no longer married, the matter of physical closeness can become a major concern. Hopefully the sexual relationship you had with your spouse was healthy and satisfying. However, even if it wasn't, at least you know that God created the sexual relationship to be a beautiful experience with its potential for intimacy and ecstasy.

One's sexuality isn't limited, however, to being physical with a partner. It affects every aspect of your being—how you think, feel, approach problems, establish relationships, and develop a self-concept. Sexuality is an integral part of who you are. You may be anywhere on the continuum from being very comfortable and fulfilled as a woman or a man to feeling frustrated or ashamed of your sexuality. Being comfortable with yourself and your sexuality is a necessary component to being fulfilled as a human being.

From the time of puberty, we also become aware of the power and pervasiveness of our sexual appetite. We all experience to some extent the involuntary attraction to another person. Physical contact (touching, holding hands, hugging, etc.) can "turn on" our sexual desire even if the contact is casual or accidental. Our imaginations can trigger sexual arousal, perhaps fueled by the media or other stimuli. This sexual desire and response mechanism is all part of God's original perfect creation. The arousal and the appetite are not sin—this is how God made us.

77

But God also put boundaries around our sexuality. "Becoming one flesh" is clearly portrayed in the Bible as the deepest relationship between a man and a woman. According to the Bible, intercourse is reserved for those who are in a lifelong committed marital relationship. Fornication (sexual intercourse outside that committed relationship) and adultery (extramarital affairs) are expressly forbidden. Our sexual desire is not like our appetite for food, allowing us to indulge in a smorgasbord of options. Just as we are to choose to serve the Lord with all our heart, soul, and mind, those who are married are also called to remain sexually faithful exclusively to their marriage partner.

So does this mean that once you become an unmarried adult because of a spousal death or divorce, you must remain sexually frustrated for the rest of your life? Not so. There are many ways to deal with your sexuality that are appropriate while maintaining your beliefs and values. For example, in a healthy courtship, you can find some level of sexual satisfaction through kissing, cuddling, or other forms of appropriate physical contact. But if you are not able to manage your sexuality at a less-expressive level, the Bible encourages you to consider remarriage in order to enjoy your sexuality within the context of marriage.

However, even if marriage is a person's choice, it is not an option for everyone because many times people are not able to find a suitable partner. You then need to find some other way to celebrate and embrace your sexual nature as a man or a woman by sublimating or redirecting it. Enjoy heterosexual relationships in a social context. Remember fondly the satisfying sexual experiences you may have had in your previous marriage. The challenge is to develop a plan to manage your sexuality so that you can remain in control of it rather than having your sexual desires begin to rule your life and compromise your integrity.

4

the second time around

Things You Need to Know about Dating and Remarriage

Gary's Journal: I'm really confused. When my wife was dying, the thought of marrying someone else was unimaginable. But over the last few months, especially since I met Eleanor, my spirit (and body!) feel like they are coming alive again. When she touched my hand for the first time, it felt like an electric shock. I'd like to date her and get to know her better. And who knows, maybe eventually marry her. But I am also concerned about what my kids will say regarding this new development. They may think I didn't love their mother.

Stacey's Journal: Can I do it again? I don't know. A lot of people still look at me as a loser, as if I couldn't make a marriage work. Oh, I know that I did some stupid things, but so did he. That's no one else's business. We basically decided that life would be easier for both of us if we just ended the marriage. Actually, I'm surprised at how well the joint custody is working. But over the last two months since I met Ben, I am really beginning to wonder if I want to do it all over again. Ben is so different from my first husband. We're dating—going out two, sometimes three, times a week. We have fun together, but I'm not sure I know him well enough yet, and I'm still learning things about myself!

Lessons Learned from Before

If your spouse died, you have gotten through the most difficult life stressor you will ever have to face. Losing a spouse through divorce is the second most stressful life experience primarily because of the need to completely reorganize your life and deal with the sense of failure in not having your marriage work.[3] After these stressful life experiences, whether you are contemplating dating again or on the brink of remarriage, we suggest setting aside a specific time and finding a quiet place to journal about what you contributed to and detracted from your previous marriage. Also consider what you have already worked on and what still needs more of your attention. Although the idea of journaling may sound tedious and unnecessary, doing this will not only validate your thoughts and feelings about your former marriage but also clarify what you would do differently in a possible future relationship. Of course, you will want to review your criteria list of what you want or don't want in a partner as discussed in chapter 3. You may also want to peruse the marriage self-help section in a bookstore or go on the web to clarify the factors necessary to make a marriage healthy and successful, things like honesty, trust, commitment, and a similar belief/faith system. Then you can combine various experts' advice with your personal preferences. Going through this process will help increase your self-esteem and self-confidence.

We also recommend you ask close and trusted friends about how they assessed your past marriage. While their opinions are no more valid than your own, they may identify some issues you might not have focused on in the same way or serve to reinforce your own perceptions. If there is no one whose opinions you trust, or even if you have already received some feedback, consider scheduling a few appointments with a counselor who specializes in relationship and marital work to help you identify areas still needing attention. All of this is aimed at going into your dating experiences and potentially next marriage (if you are considering that) with your eyes wide open, aware of what constitutes a healthy marriage. Don't be blinded by emotion. Learn to grow from your past experiences.

Words for the Widowed

Hopefully you are able to look at your past marriage realistically. Over time, working intentionally on grieving allows you to honor the good things of your marriage and take your deceased spouse off the pedestal you may have placed him or her on during the early months of widowhood. A relatively small percentage of people never stop sanitizing their marriage and continue to behave as if their deceased spouse had been a saint. This is sad because it's then extremely difficult to put the deceased in the past, reframe one's loss, and let go of the previous marriage in order to move on in a healthy way, even without choosing to remarry. Your own sense of value and worth will diminish if you think your previous spouse was better than you are. If you plan to remarry at some point, your new marriage has a higher risk of failure if you haven't recognized your deceased spouse as fully human and are able to honestly describe the negative as well as the positive characteristics of that person. A new partner could never measure up to a deceased saint.

On the other hand, if your marriage wasn't healthy, you may not have sanitized the memory of your deceased spouse. You may have lived with a spouse who was abusive, addicted, ambivalent, conflicted, or controlling, and you felt relief (maybe with a twinge of guilt) when he or she died. You may have even been contemplating separation or divorce prior to his or her death. If that is your situation, you might benefit from reading the following section on Words for the Divorced.

Words for the Divorced

Can you believe you have actually come full circle? You were once single, then married, divorced, and now single again—and at this point you may now be ready to date and begin the whole cycle again. You may actually be excited about an opportunity to be successful in marriage the next time around. At the same time, that excitement might be laced with some fear that your next relationship may also fail.

To decrease your anxieties about dating and remarriage, you need to develop a balanced view of your previous partner even if your divorce was traumatic or conflictual. Certainly your partner wasn't perfect, but he or she likely had some good points. When you begin to date, watch for the rebound effect in trying to replace or compensate for areas in your previous spouse that were intolerable and unhealthy. If you find someone in whom those weaknesses are absent, you may be blind to other potential problems. For example, if your previous spouse abused alcohol, make certain that person doesn't have a similar problem, but the absence of that problem doesn't automatically make that person acceptable as a future spouse. Keen discernment combined with time and a variety of other experiences will help you decide if this person is good for you or not. You do not want to "settle," so be deliberate and critical in your approach. Remember, you don't have to get married again. Remarriage would be wonderful only if your criteria are met.

Six Things to Assess as You Deal with Your Past When Seriously Dating Each Other

Having come out of a previous marriage, you may be tempted to make comparisons between your previous spouse and the person you are dating. Hopefully you have honestly summarized the positives and negatives of your previous marriage and know what you would like to have and do differently if you should marry again. So as you begin to date, assess the following six important things regarding this new person entering your life by having meaningful conversations together and using keen observational skills.

1. Ask your date about any previous marriage(s) and serious dating relationships fairly soon after you meet. If he or she avoids the issue or is vague or unwilling to talk about it, be on guard. Typically if someone has honestly reflected about their previous relationships, they will be able and willing to talk openly about them. Remember that both parties contributed to and need to take some responsibility for what occurred in prior dating relationships and marriages.

2. If the person you are dating has been married more than once, make certain you hear about all the marriages and what caused them to end. Find out what this person learned from each of these experiences. The more relationship failures, the more cause you have for concern.

3. Your date will also want to know about your previous marriage(s) and serious dating relationships. Hopefully you have analyzed your own experiences and are willing to talk about them candidly. Be cautious if your dating partner does *not* ask or shows little interest in your marital and dating history.

4. Ask as many questions as you can about his or her other social relationships, dates, and friendships apart from marriage. Keep that topic open-ended since you will continue to learn more about the person as you proceed in your dating relationship.

5. If the person you are dating has never been married and is already in his or her late thirties or older, you may have reason for concern. Many young people are wisely choosing to wait a while to get married, but hopefully the person you date will have had some experience with serious relationships in the past. Talk together about how he or she has dealt with close relationships and why this person has never married. This will give you some insight into his or her level of self-awareness about relationship dynamics and how suitable this person may be for a partnered relationship.

6. You would also benefit from talking about your past and present relationship with former in-laws and their extended family. If you are widowed, your in-laws might think you are being disloyal to their deceased son or daughter if you date. If you are divorced, your previous spouse's family may blame you and conclude that you were the one who didn't want to work on your marriage with their son or daughter. Hopefully you will be able to deal with any sense of awkwardness, hurt, or rejection if they resist your dating. They may not be reacting as much to you as to the grief they are still experiencing from the death or divorce. Some in-law families are able to make the transition along with you and maintain a relationship in meaningful ways. Your future relationship with them will obviously be different, particularly if you remarry. In that case, you will most likely have a new set of in-laws who then need to take precedence in your life.

Words for the Widowed

Many widowed people want to date someone who was also widowed, and frequently that new relationship works out well. But be careful, as we have been saying, not to give a person carte blanche approval just because he or she was widowed. Remember always to explore two important concerns in dating someone new: first, has this person completed the grief process with a realistic (not sanitized) memory of their former spouse; and second, how healthy was this person's marriage to their deceased partner? Be aware that dating someone who is still actively grieving is very problematic and risky. You also don't want to learn too late in the dating process that the person's prior marriage was a miserable one. You'll want time to determine exactly what contributed to that negative outcome before proceeding further.

Dating someone who was divorced presents a different challenge because that person did not have a positive experience with marriage—at least not in its final phase. There will likely be a major disparity between what both of you say about your previous spouses. A divorced person may not like to hear how happy your former marriage was. And because your dating partner did not have a successful marriage, he or she may not want to talk about the issues and failures that led to the divorce. Some divorced people want to wipe the slate clean and not talk about the past at all. Be careful about getting involved with someone who slams the door on their marital past and is unwilling to discuss or deal with pertinent issues.

Also pay attention to a divorced person's ongoing relationship with his or her ex-spouse, especially if he or she has children at home or shares custody. Some ex-spouses may try to micromanage the children even at their former spouse's home, withhold visitation, or expect inappropriate help from their ex-spouse. Dating a divorced person with dependent children may add some financial concerns. That person will potentially need to pay child support and perhaps alimony if he or she has a higher income than the ex-spouse, which could impact your future joint income and your financial security if you were to marry.

Words for the Divorced

You may want to read some of the preceding section for Words for the Widowed if as a divorced person you date someone who was widowed. Our word of warning is similar to what we wrote to the widowed person—don't assume anything based solely on the status of "widowed." Don't presume a widowed person had a healthy marriage and knows how to have an intimate relationship. Talk about it with him or her. However, remember that no one has a perfect marriage—not even someone who was widowed. Make certain he or she has realistically and honestly appraised their former marriage. Dating someone who had been happily married may be an asset as long as he or she isn't arrogant about it or doesn't attempt to control your relationship because of past success in marriage.

You may have wanted to turn your marriage around, go for counseling, or set different boundaries with your partner. Using those avenues might have worked if your partner had been willing to cooperate. We agree with the adage "it takes two to tango" and realize some relationships don't work no matter how hard you may have tried. If that was your situation, you may be afraid to date someone who initiated a divorce even if he or she now claims to have changed earlier destructive habits. Determine the degree to which the person you want to date was involved in the breakup of their past marriage. If that person had a high level of culpability, be cautious. People can make significant changes based on their experiences, reflections, counseling, and other insights, but you need to be certain that this person is worth taking that risk.

Seven Things to Talk Through before You Say "I Do"

You may be falling in love again and believe this person is the right one for you. You've dated each other for a significant period of time (we recommend exclusively for at least one year), gotten to know each other well, and now want to move toward marriage.

Prior to discussing the seven things to talk through before you say "I do," make certain you and your prospective partner have developed effective communication skills essential for a healthy relationship. We already described our view of what healthy communication looks like in the Three *P*s Regarding Dating section in chapter 3. If you are seriously considering marriage, you and your partner should feel comfortable discussing any difficult issue, feel listened to by the other person, and have developed a communication style that is balanced between the two of you. You deserve to be respected and valued—not only for your unique personality but also for your thoughts, opinions, beliefs, and feelings. But too often we hear "I didn't dare ask that or bring up that topic," or "I thought it would just work out later," or "I believed I could change my partner's attitude or behavior after we were married." No one can change another person. You may feel awkward saying something like "I have a problem with . . ." followed by giving your own opinion. But you can't work toward making mutual decisions if you don't get your own thoughts, values, and beliefs on the table. If you haven't made much progress with your dating partner in developing effective communication skills, consider seeing a counselor or attending a premarriage weekend retreat to learn healthier methods to talk with each other, make decisions together, and resolve conflicts.

Before you agree to marry each other, talk through any issues you may have in each of the following seven categories. How well you work through these will test your communication skills and display how well the two of you can resolve differences.

1. *To what degree do you share interests and activities and want to develop social relationships?* People get married not only because they love each other but also because they want to become intimately connected emotionally and physically. One key factor in developing emotional intimacy is sharing joint interests. Do you like doing similar things in your spare

time together? We recommend making a list of those interests and activities in a variety of areas that the two of you like doing as a couple. Every time you participate in an activity together you build more of a shared history that creates a solid foundation for a fulfilling marriage.

A second factor that enhances closeness is how you build your social network together. You probably both developed your own personal network of family and friends since your previous marriages ended. Dating provides an opportunity not only to know a person individually but also to observe him or her in social interactions with others. Seeing how this person responds to various situations with family and friends can either affirm your decision to proceed toward marriage or raise a shadow of doubt and concern. Explore this person's past social patterns as well. How someone has dealt with his or her social environment before you entered the picture likely represents that person's natural tendencies in social relationships. You are aware, we're sure, that people have differing degrees of interest in socializing with others. If the person you are dating has a level of social interest similar to your own, your relationship will be more compatible and require less work or compromise. A sign of a healthy dating relationship is being able to reach an agreement amicably about socializing: With whom? How often? Doing what?

On the other hand, you will also want to decide as a couple how much time each of you will socialize by yourself with your own personal friends. You may enjoy golfing, or being a part of a bowling league, or getting together with a group of your own friends on a regular basis. Discussing how this will work as a married couple is important. Depending on the extent of prior involvement, some of these individual interests may need to be reduced, eliminated, or now include your potential marriage partner. Retaining some individual activities and interests can be important to a healthy marriage, but they should not take precedence over developing joint interests and activities that will bind you closer together.

2. *Where will you live?* You will need to decide where to live after you are married. We think the healthiest scenario is that both of you leave your present residences and find a new place to live that suits the two of you. Moving into one or the other's home can be a challenge, particularly if that home was shared with a previous spouse. However, sometimes moving into a totally new place simply isn't practical, primarily for financial reasons. One of you may have dependent children living with you and want to maintain the stability of the same home at least for the time being. Or you may both really like the home or location that one of you has and want to remodel or redecorate it to meet your joint tastes. The critical factor is that you both need to agree and be sensitive to each other's wants and needs in the decision-making process.

3. *How will you manage both your own personal and joint finances?* When two people marry for the first time, they generally bring very few assets to the marriage. But when marrying for a second time (or more), you probably have accumulated some type of estate. You may also have received a life insurance settlement if you were widowed. On the other hand, if you received a pension from your deceased spouse's trust or former employment, you may be in danger of losing it when you remarry. If you were divorced, you may have to pay child support and/or alimony, or you may receive these payments to support your living expenses. You may have a large debt to deal with by yourself. Countless other scenarios could be mentioned, but our point is that by the time you decide to marry again, your financial situation will probably be quite complex.

You may want to protect your assets (such as investments, property, vehicles, etc.) through your will or a trust to give legal rights to surviving family members at your death. This is especially important if you have children from a previous marriage. After ensuring that your new spouse will be provided for throughout his or her lifetime, you can retain access to your assets by using these legal instruments and reserve whatever is left for your biological heirs. You can amend your will and trust as the need arises.

Deciding how each of you will contribute financially to your new marriage takes some negotiation. If your assets are fairly equal, you might use a three-tiered approach: yours, mine, and ours. With this approach, both of you contribute equal shares to the joint account periodically to cover your joint living expenses—food, housing costs, insurances, entertainment, etc.—while maintaining individual accounts for your personal expenses, like clothing or individual hobbies and interests.

A second option is for each of you to put whatever earnings you may have in the joint account and keep only your prior assets in individual accounts. Once you are married, whatever is earned by either one of you, even if one of you may make significantly more than the other or one person has no income, is considered by most states as joint property. We think this second option is preferable since it reflects that you are really in this marriage together, even financially. Newly remarried couples often begin with the first option and, as the level of trust between them grows, move to the second.

Both of you should decide individually which option (or some variation on those themes) you feel most comfortable with and then jointly arrive at a money management plan, including a budget for managing income and expenses. If you haven't worked with a specific budget before, check out the self-help financial resources at your local bookstore.

Here are a number of other financial suggestions to consider:

- We already suggested that you protect the assets you accumulated prior to your remarriage and not include them in joint property. In time you may be tempted to use these funds for your own daily and weekly personal interests and activities. But consider keeping these assets only for individual big ticket items, like a major personal purchase or a trip. If the two of you want to make a major joint purchase or take a trip together, you can either withdraw equal amounts from your personal accounts or make the purchase from your joint account.

- We recommend that you budget a monthly allowance from your joint money for each of you to use for your personal wants and needs. The amount should be sufficient to cover your monthly individual purchases, like entertainment or lunches with friends, or to accumulate for a larger personal purchase such as clothing, sports equipment, or a weekend trip. Clearly stipulate what personal expenses come from your allowances and which ones come from your joint budget.

- You should agree on a limit that you can spend on a joint household expense without the other person's prior approval. This may be as little as $25.00 or $50.00 depending on your budget and monthly cash flow. If you don't set a limit, you run the risk of creating a conflict over some expenditure or wreak havoc with your budget.

We recommend a prenuptial agreement to cover a wide variety of contingencies for your marriage, but make sure that you include all your financial arrangements. As you draw up this agreement, consult an attorney for guidelines on the wording and content that will be honored in a court of law. Drawing up a prenuptial in no way suggests that you don't think the marriage will last. Undoubtedly you plan on this marriage being a satisfying lifelong commitment as you grow old together. But as you already know, death and divorce do occur and can wipe out even your best-laid plans.

4. *What effect will this marriage have on your employment and career?* One of you may have the option to quit work and become a full-time homemaker, perhaps to begin a family or raise your existing children. Or one of you may want to pursue further education or training to qualify for a

more desirable job that provides more stable employment and financial security. Perhaps your work was a source of tension between you and your previous spouse. Your job may have involved a lot of travel or required you to work the second or third shift. Or you may have made work a high priority and spent more time than is healthy at your job. Your new marriage may motivate you to find a more suitable job to give your relationship a chance to flourish. If you are retired, work may not be an issue at all unless you think one or both of you might want a part-time job to provide for some of the extras in your budget.

5. *What level of physical and mental health and sexual functioning do each of you bring into the marriage?* You should both provide full disclosure of your physical and mental health history. Make certain each of you includes the history of your family of origin with respect to these issues as well. Then, you need to honestly evaluate any physical or mental health issues that either of you might have that would impair your relationship.

Most of us likely have minor physical health issues to deal with—perhaps limitations of your capacities or medications to maintain your health. Diseases like diabetes or maintaining a pacemaker can affect the quality of your life together, so you will have to discuss the impact of these issues on your future marriage.

Be cautious of a potential partner who doesn't seek treatment for a physical problem or refuses to get a second opinion for any challenging health issue. Know what he or she faces physically or emotionally; assess his or her level of investment in achieving the maximum amount of function and stability; and determine your ability and desire to cope with any abnormality before saying "I do."

Another important issue to consider is your interest in and capacity for sexual functioning. We strongly encourage you, regardless of your sexual histories, to get STD and HIV testing and share the reports with each other before you get married. This can be easily and inexpensively done at most public health departments around the country. You may think this is unnecessary, but sometimes a partner doesn't know what he or she carries. As you know, HIV can be contracted in ways other than through sexual intercourse, or he or she may be infected because of a previous partner's sexual relationships as well. Hopefully your dating partner is honest about his or her past sexual activities, but play it safe. If your partner is aboveboard and healthy, he or she should have no problem taking these precautions with you.

Additionally, share any sexual functioning problems you may have with each other. Don't surprise your partner with a physical malfunction such as impotence, a lack of sexual desire, or some other problem after you are married. Be up front now, and hopefully the two of you can work through any of these issues before marriage.

Along with sharing your physical health matters, you will also want to discuss any type of emotional or mental disorder either of you may experience. If the person you are dating has an emotional or mental disorder, you will want to assess how responsibly he or she handles that and to what extent it affects daily life. Any denial of the diagnosis or unwillingness to effectively deal with an aspect of mental illness can potentially cause problems in a marriage. The treatment for several mental health diagnoses combine medication with psychotherapy, so if your dating partner refuses to get adequate help for a treatable problem, you need to question his or her motivation to be as healthy as possible. That resistance certainly needs to be considered seriously before marriage. You will also want to know how well your potential partner is able to deal with any mental health issues you may have. If his or her response is judgmental and discounting rather than supportive, you may want to reassess the feasibility of your relationship.

6. *How compatible are your spiritual values, beliefs, life purposes, and practices?* Hopefully as you explore "Who

am I now?" following your divorce or the death of your spouse, you will also review your values, religious beliefs, and life purposes. If you embrace a specific faith perspective, you will definitely want to find out how compatible your partner's belief system is with yours. If they are similar, you can explore how you want to practice your faith as a couple through such things as worshiping together, doing volunteer work, mentoring a young person or couple, or helping those who are socially or economically challenged. Sharing similar values, religious beliefs, and working together to make a difference in some small way in the world can create a stronger bond and a sense of spiritual intimacy. If spirituality or religious practice is not important to one of you but it is to the other, you need to decide how you want to deal with that.

7. *How will you manage your individual families, especially the children?* When two people remarry, that marriage affects many other people as well, with children requiring the most consideration due to the significance of the parental bond. So discussing parenting approaches (especially for those still living at home) is critical in the dating process. You will also want to talk about the kind of relationship you both want to have with adult children. The level of closeness you each experienced in your own family of origin is significant because that influences how you will likely act, to some extent, in your new family relationships. Actually talk about your past history as a child and adolescent. More will be said about parenting concerns in chapters 6 and 7.

We would also encourage you to talk about those other family members and relatives, including former in-laws, that you have in your life and to what extent you want to be involved with them. Set a goal to develop a plan for how the two of you will deal with the many significant people in both of your lives. Remember that the more you connect jointly as a couple with them, the more you affirm the closeness of your marriage.

If in talking through each of these seven categories you discover some things that make moving ahead with the relationship problematic, be courageous and assertive enough to clarify whatever the issue(s) is. If it is major to you, you will need to try to work through it, and if you can come to no satisfactory conclusion, you will need to decide if you want to proceed with the relationship.

my spiritual journey in considering dating and remarriage

What does the Bible say about marital love? Can love be better than it was before?

Many people have a healthy and satisfying marriage in spite of all the talk about dysfunctional marriages and divorce. If you had a good marriage, and are now widowed, you may wonder if it is even possible to develop a deep, satisfying, and healthy marriage with someone else. What may raise concern is the message heard in some Christian circles that God has only *one* right person for you. And there are previously widowed or divorced people who say that they have "settled" for the companionship of a second marriage, suggesting that this marriage was second best.

Can you love again—as deeply or even more deeply than before? The answer in the Bible is a resounding yes. Let's look at what it teaches about love and how it comes to expression in marriage.

The Bible talks about two distinct but important kinds of love. *Eros* is a natural, healthy love based on mutuality. You love another person, and that person loves you back. *Agape* is Christian love that loves another without regard to the "lover's" own needs or interests. The apostle Paul combines these two types of love in Ephesians 5. He starts with mutual eros love saying that we ought to submit mutually to one another out of reverence to Christ. Did you catch the key

95

word—*mutually* submit? Each one contributes what he or she can to the relationship. But Paul goes on to say that wives should be subject to their husbands *and* husbands should sacrifice themselves for their wives just as Christ sacrificed himself for the church, which is really agape love. Think of it this way. Healthy marital love requires two distinct elements combined into one experience just as hydrogen and oxygen combine to make water. Each kind of love is unique, important, and essential in itself. But when combined, they form an entirely new experience called marital love.

If you have loved like this before, can you do it again? Or if you never experienced this kind of love, might you be able to do it now? Of course you can. As long as you know the formula and are willing to work on it together, you can certainly not only "fall" in love (which is mostly eros love) but also decide to love (which is primarily agape love) so that you and your new partner can grow together into a deeper and more satisfying love than perhaps what you may ever have experienced before.

What does the Bible say about a Christian marrying a non-Christian?

We have already encouraged you and your dating partner to consider the degree to which you are spiritually compatible. If you are both Christians but from different traditions, such as Catholic and Methodist, talk about how you will handle the differences in your traditions. Worship styles, the degree and nature of involvement in one's faith community, and how one celebrates sacraments or engages in other religious rituals can vary significantly within the Christian faith. In those cases, you will want to find a workable solution that meets both of your spiritual needs.

But what if you have met someone who doesn't share your religious beliefs, someone who may be of an entirely different non-Christian tradition or espouses no particular religious belief at all? The question here is whether or not a Christian should purposely marry a non-Christian. This isn't as unlikely a situation as you may suppose. Finding a suitable mate after having been previously married isn't necessarily an easy venture. You may find yourself attracted to someone whose faith tradition differs significantly from yours but who is quite compatible with you in many other ways.

On the one hand, the answer to the question "Should a Christian marry a non-Christian?" is quite clear. The apostle Paul specifically says in 2 Corinthians 6:14–15 that Christians are not to "be yoked together with unbelievers," and he follows that with "What does a believer have in common with an unbeliever?" This answer may seem harsh and narrow-minded to some, but we would be remiss by trying to soften it.

On the other hand, what is more important is that we come to understand why Paul would say this and ask if such a restriction still applies to Christians today. The situation at the time of Paul's writing was defined as the birth of the Christian church. Obviously most believers (if not all of them) converted to Christianity from some other religious tradition. Paul was being very clear that in a relationship as intimate as marriage, people should share the same common beliefs and values. We think this principle still applies today.

Think of it this way. If you and your new partner disagree about what kind of music each of you might like, or if one wants to go to a hockey game while the other prefers to go to a movie, you can certainly find a way to compromise or accommodate without violating the very core or essence of who you are (or that of the other person). One's religious commitment, however, is a "heart" matter—a faith commitment that lies at the very core of one's being. The Christian faith isn't just one of several options as a matter of personal choice. Deep faith values direct our lives and contribute to a sense of integrity. Any significant difference between the two of you in the area of religious belief guarantees that you will have major points of tension as you live and love together.

We have encouraged you to analyze the degree of compatibility you have on a number of levels—social interests, residence, finances, work, and spiritual aspects. We firmly believe that spiritual compatibility is foundational to a healthy, intimate marriage and is critical in developing your life's meaning, purposes, and future together.

5

in our own words

A Sequel to "The Second Time Around"

Each of the preceding chapters contained separate sections entitled "Words for the Widowed" and "Words for the Divorced" to specifically address the differences with both types of spousal loss. We are changing the format here to share our personal insights as authors who have gone through the experience of being widowed and then eventually dating, remarrying, and blending our families. Each of our adult children also contributed by responding to a set of questions about their experience of watching us date, fall in love, marry, and blend our families over the past thirteen years. While this is our personal story, and your story may differ significantly from ours, we hope you will be able to glean some help and support from our experiences.

Through Our Eyes as Widowed

Susan's Perspective on Beginning Again

"Rick, my first husband, died after eighteen years of struggling with a malignant brain tumor. While processing the reality of his predicted death over those years, we talked about many difficult things. He frequently told me to remarry after he died. I was repulsed at the thought. We had a very good marriage, and I didn't like the idea of perhaps contaminating my memories with a negative experience with someone else. After he died, and as I journeyed through my grief, the idea of having another marital relationship remained nauseating for quite some time. I didn't believe remarriage would be an option even if I changed my mind because, as several people didn't hesitate to tell me, my expectations of what a marital partner would need to be were far too idealistic. However, once I finished grieving, I began to think more positively about dating, but I determined I would never 'settle' for another partner. If I were to remarry, that person would have to meet all my criteria. I had previously written a list of the qualities and characteristics I would require in another person, and what I could not tolerate if I were to consider remarriage. Before beginning to attend singles' activities, I talked with my daughter, parents, and former in-laws to let them know I was feeling open and ready to date if that opportunity ever presented itself."

Bob's Perspective on Beginning Again

"I don't think I ever *decided* to date. Actually, before Susan and I met, I had no desire to date and had turned down several social invitations that looked like a date to me. Char and I had a good marriage. Like Rick did for Susan, Char had encouraged me to date and possibly marry again. But the thought of getting into another relationship was totally unappealing even after working through my grief. I couldn't imagine doing better the second time around. Besides, I had gotten to the point of enjoying and appreciating the flexibility that being single allowed. So when Susan and I met, I had no intention of moving into a romantic relationship. I was excited about our interest to write a book together, compiling our experiences of how each of us had traveled the grief journey. In the process of writing, we also became good friends. Both of us from the start had determined not to consider dating anyone until we were through grieving. I realized along the way, however, that we were developing a close relationship and that someday I might eventually want to date and perhaps marry her."

Susan's Perspective on the Dating Process

"I was fortunate that my marriage to Rick turned out so well, being only twenty-two when we married and rather naive about what to expect. In dating the second time around (after having been married for more than twenty-four years), I had a better sense of who I was and what was important to me. I approached dating with much more confidence and a higher level of self-esteem. Bob and I met when I had been widowed only seven months. By the time I finished grieving, shortly after the anniversary of Rick's death, Bob expressed an interest to be more than friends and try dating. I really thought a great deal of him so I was intrigued at the prospect. However, I also thought it wise to check out the single world through a variety of singles' activities and other dating opportunities in addition to dating him. I did not rush into anything, and I wanted to be as objective as possible. When on a date I asked questions important to me, and when the answer didn't fit my identified criteria I ruled that person out as a dating possibility. The process was a good experience as I genuinely liked meeting new people while discovering what it was like to be single again. I was able to validate even more who I was and what I wanted if I were to enter another exclusive relationship. But I know that meeting Bob was definitely a result of God's hand in both our lives. My relationship with God is of extreme importance to me, and any potential partner would need to share my faith perspective. Still, I didn't bargain on falling in love with a minister from we to me

who had a high level of commitment to beliefs similar to mine. That turned out to be a real bonus."

Bob's Perspective on the Dating Process

"I still associate the term 'dating' with what I did in high school and college. During that period in my life dating was an event fairly disassociated with the rest of my life. It was something to do on Friday or Saturday night. Even after meeting Char in college, we went on Saturday night dates for a long time before it turned into a deeper relationship. With Susan, the deeper relationship was the starting point. Not only did she meet all my criteria, she exceeded them. With Susan, the relationship was immediately more authentic and rich than any dating relationship was in high school or college. The romance and passion were certainly there, but I also knew far better what I was getting into. I had never met a woman who exhibited such a passion for life, had great insights into human behavior, and was willing to color outside the lines, which had been my natural tendency all along. I think I knew I was falling in love with Susan. I remember a time about six months after our meeting telling her that my feelings for her were changing into something more romantic than just being professional colleagues or friends. I also told her she didn't have to say anything in response then, nor would I bring it up again until much later when she might be more ready to entertain that."

Susan's Perspective on the Engagement and Wedding

"Bob and I dated exclusively for about thirteen months before we were engaged. As we continued to date we increasingly talked about the possibility of getting married. We both knew we were moving in that direction. I talked with my daughter about my thoughts of remarriage. She knew Bob and I were becoming more serious, at least as much as she could as an out-of-state college student home only for holi-

102

days and school breaks. Bob and I discussed how we would make our engagement official, and at Bob's request we agreed that he would do the more traditional thing and decide when and how to propose. As it turned out, all of our kids and my parents knew about Bob's proposal before I did. He did it in grand style with a limo, dinner, a dozen roses at our table, and dancing afterwards. He had arranged a breakfast the next morning for my parents and two of his children and families who were in town so they could celebrate with us. Unfortunately, his son lived too far away to attend, and my daughter was at college about six hours away. It was extremely important to me that all of our kids were on board with our upcoming marriage, but particularly my daughter. I wanted so badly for her to make that transition with us, and I believe she has been successfully on board with the two of us pretty much from the start."

Bob's Perspective on the Engagement and Wedding

"I went away by myself for a weekend before I proposed to Susan where I wrote letters to each of my children describing how I had grieved the death of their mother, how I was now rebuilding my life, and how I was certain that my growing relationship with Susan would become permanent. I'm not sure how they felt about the letters, but writing them was extremely helpful for me. Susan described how the engagement went—at least in part. One factor that loomed large was the promise I had made to her that I not propose at a time when her daughter was away at school. That's why I arranged for us to drive to her out-of-state college the morning after we became engaged. Sarah was ready for our arrival with a huge bottle of champagne. I, of course, hoped that all the kids would be on board, but I had also gotten to the point where their approval or disapproval wouldn't be a deal breaker. This was my decision, and I recognized God's hand was on this wonderful twist in my life."

Their Kids' Perspectives on Dating and Remarriage

Susan has one daughter, and Bob has one son and two daughters. All of our children were emerging adults when our first spouses died. Bob's children were all married within the four years preceding our wedding. Susan's daughter was in college and wasn't married until seven years after we were. In writing this book, we asked each of our adult children to honestly and candidly complete a questionnaire about how they experienced our dating and remarriage. We had not asked the specific questions posed to them that directly before. We'll let them tell their stories in their own words, organized around the questions we asked.

To begin with, we wanted to know: *What did you think and how did you feel when you realized your parent was finished grieving and getting ready to move on, which might also include dating?*

Sarah was very direct in her reply. "I didn't like the idea of you dating, Mom. I thought it was too soon to be starting a new relationship. I know initially you said you were just friends with Bob, but I thought that it was more. I liked the idea of you finding someone to spend your time with, but not more than that. You might have looked at your relationship with Bob as a friendship, but from the start I looked at it as a replacement."

The idea of replacing the deceased parent is a huge issue for most children. They want to keep the memory of their parent intact, and often having someone new in the role of partner to their surviving parent is a real stretch for them.

Carrie had a different twist on the issue of dating. "I knew it would eventually happen. I found myself split down the middle. On one side I was happy for my dad—happy that he felt ready to begin again. But yet sad that this was a definite sign of him closing the chapter with my mom. I wasn't necessarily ready for it."

One of the themes that emerged with all of our children was some level of happiness that their surviving parent was moving on and finding new companionship. Brian put it this way: "I remember the first time my dad mentioned he had met a 'friend.' We were hiking in Colorado. I could tell he was excited about his new relationship. I was happy he was moving on and taking steps to begin developing a relationship again." Christy echoed something similar, saying: "I think I was happy to see him at a place where he could continue to live his life and have the possibility of meeting someone to share the rest of his life with."

We followed that by asking: *What were your feelings and reactions when you first realized that your dad/mom was beginning to develop a dating relationship? What was it like for you when you met Susan/Bob for the first time? How did your feelings and reactions change, if at all, when you began to realize that their relationship was developing into something more than "just friends"?*

Brian touched on two rather common reactions—initial happiness for his dad mixed with some anxiety about what this might mean for him and his sisters. "My feelings were quite neutral when meeting Susan. However, they became mixed when I began to realize their relationship was more serious than 'just friends.' I had felt a bit relieved that Dad was able to develop a relationship with someone and talk about things that were important to him. But I was also a bit concerned for selfish reasons about what dating would do to my relationship with my dad. Would he change? Would he still be interested in what I was doing? How would it affect the dynamics of our family?"

Christy and Carrie had nearly the same reaction as Brian. Christy said: "I remember being happy for him. He had a whole new look about him. But meeting Susan for the first time was a bit awkward because I was seeing my dad with another woman. She seemed nice, and I know Dad was excited to have us meet her. I was happy that Dad had someone to go out and have fun with, but it was also hard to realize that he was moving on and that his life with my mom was truly over. It was exceptionally difficult when he sold our childhood home, which was good for him, but was another indication that he was moving forward."

Carrie added: "I don't think the friendship bothered me so much. I anticipated that at some point my dad was going to start to develop new friendships. I do recall being very upset with my dad's timing in telling me he was going to date Susan. I was studying for a big exam the next day and couldn't concentrate after that. I know I wasn't too elated about meeting Susan for the first time. I remember feeling more awkward anxiety and don't think my feelings changed much as my dad and Susan initially got more serious."

Susan's daughter, Sarah, had the dilemma of maybe liking the new person in her mom's life but being anxious about how this was all going to impact her. "Meeting Bob for the first time was strange, but I thought he was a nice guy and liked him from the start. What I didn't like was that when I couldn't find something in the kitchen he knew right where it was. I was so far away and removed from their relationship that it really didn't bother me to realize the relationship was becoming more than 'just friends.' I was glad my mom was happy. I wasn't thinking about him as a new dad but more as a new hubby for my mother."

Obviously, one of the biggest challenges we faced as we became increasingly aware that we were falling in love and might eventually marry was finding a balance between nurturing our developing relationship while dealing honestly with the impact it would have on our emerging adult children. This was especially challenging because, while we were convinced we were through our grieving, our children were still dealing with their own grief regarding the death of their parent.

To follow up with that we asked: *What was it like for you to see your dad/mom begin a new relationship while you were still grieving your mom's/dad's death?*

For Sarah, our developing relationship was difficult to watch. "I didn't like the PDA (public display of affection) at all. I didn't remember seeing you, Mom, behaving that way with my dad. It made me really uncomfortable. I felt like you were throwing your relationship in my face, which, at the time, I wasn't ready for because I was still dealing with the loss of my dad."

Brian's response concerned seeing his dad looking different than before his mother's death. "At first it wasn't a big deal, but as the relationship developed, Dad was doing more things with Susan, going more places, and living life like I hadn't seen before. That part was a bit more difficult because I had not seen him that happy. So questions started to enter my mind. Had I ever seen him this happy with my mom? Did he miss my mom? Some of his behaviors started to change. I realized Dad was going through a rebirth. My dad as I knew him was not going to be the same as when he was married to my mom. I was happy for him, but I was also scared as to how it would affect me and my relationship with him."

Children want to know that their surviving parent loved their deceased parent and was grateful for the marriage with him or her. And they need to learn that it's not disloyal in the least for their surviving parent to want to move on and develop a new volume in their life. After all, a person can't be disloyal to someone who has died and is no longer here.

We know that a young adult's wedding day can be a time for reflection and possible sadness after a parent has died. With that in mind, we asked the question: *What was it like for you on your wedding day when your dad/mom wasn't there and your other parent was moving (or had moved) into a new relationship?*

Christy was the first one to get married, a year and a half after her mother's death. "My wedding day was bittersweet. I was 'over the moon' to be getting married, but it was very difficult to plan and have a wedding without my mom there. I remember how Dad stepped in and was very involved in the planning process. He did his best to fill Mom's shoes, and I think he did a great job. The hardest part of that day was right before he walked me down the aisle when we had our father-daughter moment together. His relationship with Susan was so new that I had not met her yet. As a result, she was not at our wedding, which was probably a good thing."

Carrie was married a year after Christy. Even though it was nearly three years after her mother died, the event was still quite emotional and presented a number of challenges. Here's what Carrie had to say about her wedding day: "Of course it was a wonderful day, getting married and celebrating with friends and family, but I definitely felt the absence of my mom a lot that day. I had missed being able to plan my wedding with her and everything that entails. My dad had a sale of the household contents (including my mom's things) shortly before my wedding. That was definitely hard for me. It made me think of her more and dwell on the fact that she wasn't going to be there. Dad moved out of our family home that same summer, and that loss was another hurdle I had to face."

Later that same year, Brian got married. "Susan was very supportive on my wedding day, which I greatly appreciated, but that didn't change the fact that I wanted Mom there. Her absence was on my mind a lot, but it didn't dominate my feelings for the day."

Even though Sarah was married seven years after our marriage and a full decade after her father died, her reaction to the absence of her father was quite typical for someone at these milestone events in life. She had asked Susan to walk her down the aisle, which was a bittersweet reminder that her dad couldn't be there. "It was very sad for me that my dad wouldn't be there," Sarah said. "I wasn't the kind of girl who dreamed about her wedding, but it was a big event, and I feel like he would have made it complete. I wanted him there helping me at my wedding and later getting to know who I've become as well as having a relationship with my kids. However, I loved having Bob there (he actually officiated at the wedding ceremony). He has become a father to me."

When we were planning our wedding events, we were aware of the impact this would have on our children. We wanted them on board as part of a newly blended family, and so, because we saw this as the only opportunity to all be together for quite a while, we invited Susan's parents and our children to join us for three days of our honeymoon. Our question to our kids was: *What was it like for you on your parent and stepparent's wedding day? How did you feel about being with them on a portion of their honeymoon? What would have made these events better for you?*

Sarah was quite positive about her experience. She said: "I enjoyed your wedding day, and I had a fun time on your honeymoon. At that point, I had come around to accepting our new family. I liked that I had some time to be with my new stepsibs so we could talk about everything and bond without Mom and Bob there all the time."

On the other hand, Bob's kids thought that while it was a good idea, the experience was a bit awkward for them. Brian put it this way: "Their wedding was in a beautiful setting and the service was beautiful, but I felt a little out of place. Logically and rationally, Dad getting remarried made perfect sense, but it just seemed a bit unnatural to me. I was happy for Dad and Susan since they had healed from their personal losses and were able to find new meaning and each other. The honeymoon was a nice gesture. However, the more I thought about and experienced it, the more I felt as though I was in an episode of *The Brady Bunch*. Wasn't a honeymoon for two people rather than a bunch of family? It may have been better if Dad and Susan had just gone on their honeymoon by themselves and let the rest of the blended family get to know each another on our own schedule and in our own way."

Christy and Carrie echoed each other's thoughts. Christy said: "On Dad and Susan's wedding day I was very happy for them. Dad was happy, and I could tell how much he loved and cared about Susan. The honeymoon was very generous but a bit awkward, and I felt out of place. I'm not sure that was a beneficial way to blend us." Carrie added: "We agreed to go on the honeymoon with Dad and Susan because they really wanted everyone to be there. At the same time, we didn't feel like it was an integral part of blending the families."

We agree that blending is initially difficult and awkward for most every family because merging involves two distinct family systems with different ways of organizing and doing things. Having our adult children spread geographically around the country created additional challenges. Our entire new family can get together only occasionally on holidays or other special occasions, so those were the times we tried to plan events to which all the kids were invited. We surmise that if they had all lived closer to us and each other, the blending might have been easier. Because we felt it was so important that everyone have an equal opportunity to get on board, and two of our kids were flying back to their homes out of state following our wedding, we offered the invitation to spend a few days with us on Mackinac Island. We also realized that because our children were young adults, a majority of their personal investment and focus was directed toward establishing their careers and growing relationships with spouses and/or dating partners, leaving less energy to connect with each other. We weren't at all convinced they would be motivated to exert energy into becoming a blended family in their own way unless we took the initiative.

Of course, these comments represent *our* family's experiences and are not presented as the perfect model or necessarily the most effective or only way to handle things for you. But hopefully these glimpses into our lives will help you see what the movement from dating to remarriage was like for us, and our experiences can give you some things to ponder and use on your own journey.

Through the Eyes of the Divorced

Since neither of us has been divorced, we asked our good friends Ed and Jean and their children[4] to share their personal experiences of blending their families. Both divorced from their previous spouses, they met each other and were married around the same time we were. Ed has two daughters, and Jean has two sons and one daughter. Their children answered a number of questions about their reactions to Ed and Jean meeting, dating, marrying, and blending their new family. Your story will be different from theirs because each is unique, but hopefully you will find the contents helpful for you.

Jean's Perspective on Beginning Again

"I did not grieve the divorce itself but rather grieved the failure of my first marriage, which wasn't good from the beginning. Actually I grieved the loss of that marriage for years, finally drumming up the courage to divorce with the hope that maybe I could have a good marriage someday. I was still reeling from my decision to divorce when I was introduced to Ed through a friend. I wasn't really looking for another relationship. While in the process of divorcing I had journaled all the qualities and characteristics of what I was looking for, just trying to imagine what a good husband might look like. The thing that kept me in the relationship was that Ed had those characteristics that I had journaled about earlier. As I got to know him, I did talk with my children about what was going on with the two of us. My sons' responses were casual, since they were in college and totally consumed by their own lives. My daughter just seemed to trust me. The grief over the brokenness that a divorce creates hit me later, even after I was married to Ed. That brokenness of the family unit is most apparent to me at holidays, birthdays, weddings, and funerals. I believe it is through the healthy marriage I have now that healing continues to take place."

Ed's Perspective on Beginning Again

"It was not too long after the separation and divorce that I made a pretty intentional decision to date again and most likely remarry. I was nearly through my grief by that time, but certainly not completely. I think dating someone who had also been divorced actually helped me finish my grieving. My daughters thought dating was a good idea at the time; in fact, they suggested it. It was an incredibly awkward period since I had a hard time thinking of myself as a single person. When it came to finding someone who met my criteria, I had some idea of what I wanted, but more things I did not want. I didn't write anything down; it was all in my head."

Jean's Perspective on the Dating Process

"I had reached middle age by the time I got a divorce, was in a leadership role in my career, and was busy raising three children. In dating Ed, I was less emotional than the first time around or at least more in control and aware of my emotions. I had a close relationship with God, met with a wonderful Christian counselor, and had a number of amazing women friends. I felt hopeful, adventuresome, and a little bit nervous. However, I was in no hurry to remarry and figured it would take a lot longer to find the right person than it did. I believed dating Ed had the potential to change my life. One of the most important factors in my decision to date him was his commitment to his Christian faith. I prayed for discernment regarding his heart, and I believe God showed me that. We dated exclusively for about a year before we married."

Ed's Perspective on the Dating Process

"I had met my first wife while visiting former high school friends who were at college. I think our dating was mostly focused on fun and partying but not serious conversations. After divorcing, I knew I would date again. I was nervous, excited, scared, but hopeful as well when Jean and I started to date. I did not think I would be blessed in finding someone so soon. I met Jean through a mutual friend suggesting we were both in similar situations: recently divorced, both Christians, and both born on March 15. I called her on our shared birthday and made arrangements for us to meet. Dating Jean was very different from any prior experiences I had in that we had many more discussions about important topics. I felt the stakes were significantly higher with kids and all. The fact that we lived forty-five miles apart made it even more challenging. As Jean has indicated, sharing our mutual faith was a huge factor in bringing and keeping us together. My faith has always been an important component of my life. Jean's religious upbringing was different from mine, but the core issues of our faith are very similar. I knew within the first year of dating that I wanted to marry her."

Jean's Perspective on the Engagement and Wedding

"Moving toward engagement and a wedding meant we had to begin communicating with our emerging adult children about what was going on between us. After talking with my kids, we took our daughters to a baseball game together. My sons met Ed for the first time when he picked me up for a date. Those times were difficult because everyone was so uncomfortable, including me. My second son got to know Ed when he helped him move in and out of places in college. Ed was nothing but kind and accommodating. It would have been hard for them not to like him, but it took a while for them to know him. When we got closer to marriage, I told my children what was going to happen. Since Ed and his kids lived in another city, my kids were concerned that they would have to move there. So we decided to continue to live separately in our own homes for a little while after the wedding in order to honor our children's lives. Overall, my children seemed fine with the news that I was marrying Ed. They acted like it didn't matter that much to them as long as I was happy and knew what I was doing. I knew it was going to eventually make a big difference to them but chose to take their approval at face value because I thought it was right and would be blessed. It was important to me that the kids did not object to our marriage.

"Our wedding was a relatively simple event. We invited only our kids to the ceremony and dinner afterward. Deciding to involve the children was the result of many long conversations. I wanted to go away somewhere quietly and get married, but Ed wanted the kids to be there and participate in some way. In the end involving them was the best decision. I had mixed thoughts about how much or how little the children should blend in our new family. I knew blending could be painful and did not want them to think that just having them at the wedding was the solution. As Ed and I talked about this later, we realized that we each came at marriage and blending from entirely different perspectives. He was thinking of me as a second mother to his girls. On the other hand, I had no illusions that my children would want another father."

Ed's Perspective on the Engagement and Wedding

"As Jean mentioned, we were very intentional about arranging the first meeting for our respective children. We agreed that a neutral, externally focused event would be the best. I think the girls really liked Jean, especially in the beginning. They liked how she was interested in their lives. My girls were happy for me, and it was important for me that they liked Jean. I think they figured we would eventually get married since we had been dating each other exclusively for a while."

Their Kids' Perspectives on Dating and Remarriage

None of Ed and Jean's children were married at the time of their marriage. Three of them were still living at home and attending high school while the other two were away at college. You will hear in their responses some of the issues that come from joining two families with a history of divorce into one household.

We began with the following questions: *What did you think and how did you feel when you realized your parent was through dealing with the divorce and was getting ready to move on, which probably would include dating? What were your feelings and reactions when you first realized that your dad/mom was beginning to develop a friendship with someone else, and when you met Ed/Jean for the first time?* Here's what they said in their own words, replete with honesty and candor.

Gordon is Jean's oldest. You can hear the struggle early on in seeing his mom with another man: "Through the divorce I felt that her priority was that her kids would be okay, so I wanted her to be happy now. I thought she deserved that. I did feel a little strange when I learned about her dating Ed, but I didn't think she was looking for anything serious. When I first met him, I thought it was weird seeing my mom with somebody other than my dad. I wanted to be critical of Ed, but the only thing I could come up with was he was too nice."

Lisa is Jean's youngest. "At the time my parents divorced, I was a junior in high school. I felt confused, sad, and crushed. I wished my parents had worked it out and stayed together. I felt bad for my mom because my dad didn't love her anymore. When her divorce was final she seemed happier. Before she began to date I was the only child still at home so our relationship grew stronger. When I was introduced to Ed, I thought he was a nice man. But what I didn't like at first was how he, a stranger, took my mom somewhere, and I didn't know where she was going and when she'd be back."

Jean's middle child, Troy, was facing some personal challenges at the time she started dating Ed. Here's what Troy had to say: "In a word, I felt betrayed. I felt more distance between my mom and myself during that period of life than at any other time. I had little access to her grieving process so I didn't have a sense of what it meant for her to get through her divorce in order to move on. As a result, I felt abandoned, which was a significant shift from how I felt prior to the divorce. That only served to further justify my anger, bitterness, and my escape into an addictive lifestyle. So I viewed my mom beginning to date with great ambivalence. On one hand I longed for stability, and her dating seemed a potential road to that end, but on the other hand I felt sickened. The pursuit of numbness and indifference was the option I chose more often than not. But to be honest, sometimes I was glad and excited for her. For years I had been aware that my mom wanted more from my dad than he gave her, and this relationship came with new possibilities. I also felt anxious, confused, and out of the loop. When I finally met Ed for the first time, I recall vividly wanting my approval or disapproval to have meaning, but ultimately I felt small and powerless. I looked for reasons to be dismissive of him. I looked for flaws and shortcomings that would allow me to take him and their relationship less seriously. I wanted a focal point for my rage. But through it all Ed was kind and respectful, which was all the more disarming and enraging."

Reed, one of Ed's two daughters, accepted our invitation to comment on her experience with her dad marrying Jean and blending their households. To this first set of questions, Reed replied: "The idea of my dad dating was pretty horrifying to me. I think I had an idea of his need to start over, but that was quickly replaced with thoughts about me and my sister and how his social life would vastly impact ours. I really didn't learn anything about Jean from my dad prior to our first meeting. I remember her standing in the kitchen of our house, drinking a cup of coffee. My dad introduced her as his friend, although I remember thinking she was probably more than that. I thought she seemed nice enough, but she struck me as very different, dressed in her business attire, compared to my mom."

Being friends, or dating casually, is often less difficult for teen and adult children to accept than when parents begin to become serious and move toward marriage. That often triggers a number of other reactions. So we asked: *How did your feelings and reactions change, if at all, when you began to realize that your parent's relationship was developing into something more than "just friends"? What was it like for you to see your dad/mom begin a new relationship while you were likely still dealing with the reality of your parents' divorce?*

Reed was quite transparent in her response: "I think I was probably pretty self-involved in my own life, but I thought that it seemed really soon after my parents' divorce for my dad to be interested in Jean. I am sure that he waited a while before bringing her to our house, and even at that point I thought it was pretty quick."

Lisa pointed out how quickly jealousy can set in—a feeling of competition and disenfranchisement occurred as her mother became more serious with Ed. "My feelings and reactions changed when I realized my mom and Ed were more than 'just friends.' I was both happy and jealous. Happy because she appeared happy and acted like she was on cloud nine. I was jealous because Ed was starting to spend more time with her. I wanted to be with my mom more and also get to know Ed better. I had always hoped and prayed that my parents would get back together and love each other again. But I began to see the feelings my mom had for Ed, and my dad already had a new girlfriend. Knowing they were happy with their new partners, I slowly started to be okay with it all."

Jean's sons had a different reaction because they were away at college and removed from day-to-day interactions with their mom and Ed. Gordon said: "I was good with them becoming more than just friends because I saw Ed treating my mom with respect and making her happy. I was okay with my mom's new relationship, but I also spent most of my time away at college."

Troy didn't meet Ed until later in the dating relationship. He responded: "By the time I met Ed I was already aware that they were more than just friends. I knew my mom was not just looking to make new friends, and I also had a sense that she wouldn't have introduced Ed to our family if there was no potential for a serious relationship. Nevertheless, as she was moving into this relationship I was feeling more and more lonely."

Do you hear the cacophony of emotions involved in this movement? Jealousy, loneliness, relief, happiness—watching a parent go through the dating process triggers a full range of emotional responses. Following Ed and Jean's wedding, all of their children eventually married as well. Therefore, we wanted to know: *What was it like for you on your wedding day? Were both your parents and stepparents there, and if so, what did that feel like?*

Gordon simply said: "The wedding day was fine. Because they were married after I was already in college, Ed never had a parenting role with me. My dad was there as my dad, and Ed was there as my mom's husband and my friend."

Troy had the same fairly straightforward response. "On my wedding day I remained fairly disengaged from the tension of having two sets of parents present. I recall being very aware of the amount of affection I showed my dad and stepdad. I felt some responsibility to protect my dad from the potential hurt in sharing the 'dad' role."

Even Lisa, whom you might think would have a harder time as the youngest person in this blended family structure, seemed to think that her wedding went well. "On my wedding day, both my dad and stepdad were present. I loved that they both attended the most important day of my life, my wedding. I felt loved by both of them and nothing felt awkward."

Ed's daughter avoided the entire issue by not having a family wedding. "I eloped, so I can't respond to those issues. I think after my sister got married my dad was quite grateful that he had to pay for only one wedding!"

In conclusion we wondered how they now see their parent's marriage, so we asked: *Do you think it would have been preferable for your dad/mom to have remained single? What would be the advantages or disadvantages?*

Reed's response was one of happiness for her parent and a realization that she has grown through this experience. "It's hard to imagine what my dad would have done alone. When my mom and dad initially separated he had a twelve- and thirteen-year-old to look after, not an easy task, so I understand how he would want a partner to help raise two teenage girls. I think he would have been pretty miserable by himself. I believe all things happen for a reason, and no doubt this whole situation has made me the woman I am today."

Gordon's succinct response to remaining single versus remarriage was: "I think my mom did what she thought was right, and I respect her decision."

In this and the preceding chapter, we have covered a number of the issues involved in dating and dealing with remarriage. We included some of the theory and research as well as glimpses into the life stories of a widowed and a divorced remarried couple along with their respective children to give you some idea of the complexity of remarriage with children along on the journey.

We invite you now to hear the conclusion of our stories in the next two chapters, where we focus on the opportunities and challenges for those who get remarried, parent together, and work on blending their two families. However, if you have chosen to remain single following the loss of your spouse, you may opt to either continue on to chapter 6 or move directly to chapter 8 for thoughts on designing your future life. In chapter 8 we will discuss how you can be wise and deliberate about applying what you have learned from your prior experiences as you reinvest in life in exciting and rewarding ways.

6

blended or chunky

The Art of Parenting and Stepparenting

Amanda's Journal: I thought that parenting our kids went pretty well before my husband died. Now that I'm remarried, parenting has become very complicated! Sometimes Mike, my new husband, sets the rules for his two kids, and I do similarly for my three. Then there are times when he expects me to enforce his rules for all the kids—but I'm not sure his rules are best for mine. Oh, how we struggle to get this figured out to both of our satisfactions because we don't really want to have a "yours and mine" type of family. We are doing pretty well with other aspects of our relationship, but it's challenging to parent together.

Josh's Journal: Sometimes I really don't think this blending is going to work very well. My new wife, Ann, and I now have four kids together, two are adolescents and two are emerging adults. It's quickly becoming apparent that they can play us off each other and pit us against our former spouses. Holidays and birthdays are tough. The kids and families say there are too many people to see and places to go. There are just too many variables to contend with. I'm confused about how to be a close family with all the juggling of schedules needed to spend time together while also not ignoring all the other stuff I have to deal with.

Part 1: Observations about Blending a Chunky Family

Some Suggestions for the Road Ahead—Blended or Chunky

The roles, functions, and traditions of your family change when someone dies or gets divorced, underscoring the fact that this person who once was in your family is no longer sharing life with you. These changes become even more challenging when you add a new person to the family mix. Incorporating your new partner takes time and deliberate intention. Not only does he or she have to find a place within the family system, but everyone needs to adjust to one another and to different ways of doing things.

Can two families really merge into a new family? That is what you, like us, might hope for. But blending can't obliterate the individual differences and styles that existed previously in the two merging families. Attempting to puree everyone together is unrealistic and may set the stage for resistance. That is why we prefer the term "chunky," using the analogy of vegetable soup. Each individual ingredient contributes to the total flavor and texture while retaining its own identity and distinct taste. This mixing or blending needs to be done in an environment where everyone can express their opinions openly about how to organize the new chunky family, create an identity, celebrate special occasions, and enjoy family times together. Of course, the final decisions regarding how to come together and what to do as a blended family need to coordinate as well with your parental goals for becoming a healthy reconfigured family.

What Can I Do as the New Stepparent to Begin This Blending Process in a Positive Way?

If you are at all like we were, you want to be accepted and liked by your partner's children. You've been down the marriage road at least once before (maybe more). You are no longer a wide-eyed rather naive young adult. If you and your new partner each have children, the process of joining your families together won't happen quickly. Developing some level of closeness between a stepparent and stepchild as well as between stepsiblings takes patience and hard work. Building relationships can be a painstakingly slow process, and some relationships may never reach the level you hope for. But remember, the nature of the relationship that is developed does not depend only on you. Your children, regardless of their age, must be willing to reciprocate in order to build a close, caring relationship. Still, as parents you are primarily responsible, especially in the beginning years of your new marriage, to find ways to start building a healthy relationship with your stepchildren.

The following African folktale involving a boy whose mother had died helps illustrate the patience it takes to build a close relationship with stepchildren.

Sometime after his mother's death, the boy's father remarried a wonderful woman who reached out to her new stepson with respect and kindness. But the boy still grieved his mother's death and rejected his stepmother's attempts to connect with him. He said harsh words to her and defied any authority that she tried to exercise as his stepmother. She tried everything she could to get him to love her, but he rejected all her attempts. The more she pushed and prodded, the more cold and defiant he became. Nothing she did worked.

123

Finally, in desperation, the woman went to see the witch doctor as was the custom in her tribe. She told him of her resistant stepson and asked him to make a potion that she could give him so that he would like her. The old witch doctor listened to the stepmother's story and told her that first she must bring him a whisker from a ferocious mountain lion.

The stepmother was shocked and frightened by the task she had been given, but she loved her husband and wanted to be loved by her stepson, so she set out toward the mountains where the lions lived.

She soon found lion tracks that led to a cave on the side of a mountain. She quietly walked up to the mouth of the cave and took some raw meat from her sack, placing it on the ground. Then she walked a hundred steps away and hid in the bushes. The mountain lion, smelling the delicious meat, came out of the cave. He looked around for enemies, and when he saw none he devoured his tasty meal.

The woman came back the next day with more meat, which she again left at the mouth of the cave. But this time, she walked only fifty steps away and stood in the open. Each day for a week, she came back with meat. And each time, she stood a little closer to the feasting lion. Eventually, the lion ate from her hand while she gently stroked his fur. Finally, she was able to pull a whisker from his chin while he ate.

She returned to the witch doctor with the whisker she needed to make the potion that would win the affection of her rebellious and resistant stepson. But the wise old healer told her: "You do not need a potion to win the boy's heart. Instead, you must approach him in the same manner you did the untamed mountain lion—slowly and patiently."

The stepmother followed the witch doctor's advice and worked hard to get a little bit closer to her stepson every day. By the season's end, the stepson no longer treated her like a dangerous foe. For the first time, the two saw the possibility of becoming friends and living happily and lovingly together in their new stepfamily.[5]

We personally found some wisdom in this classic legend and tried to apply it to our own journey of blending our families. Sometimes when we felt frustrated or misunderstood by our children or stepchildren, we would console each other with: "Remember the lion's whisker!" The phrase reminded us of the deliberate and arduous process involved in blending two different families into a new one.

How Will I Parent My Children, My Partner's Children, and Our Joint Children?

What are some of the obstacles and challenges you may face when you begin to bring your two families together? Two overriding concerns emerge for most offspring regardless of their age. First, children typically do not want things to change from their "old normal" family, and second, they resist changes because they probably experience divided loyalties between their displaced or deceased parent and the new stepparent.

The age of your children or adolescents can impact the degree of difficulty in adjusting to a new stepparent in the home. Kids who are under twelve tend to have less trouble accepting the change and may gradually be more open to accepting a new person in their life. By the time children become adolescents, however, they seem to be more resistant primarily because they are trying to figure out their own identity and how to be accepted by peers. Teens tend to focus mostly on their own friendships and intimacy issues. They are moving away from their childhood family to figure out their place in the greater scheme of things. Working on their developmental tasks leaves little time, energy, or desire to adapt to a changing family structure that they didn't want in the first place. So, often the new partner can become the unwanted target of myriad negative feelings including resentment, dislike, anger, disinterest, or rejection.

The parent and new stepparent can help their children in this process by clarifying their hopes for the new family structure rather soon after deciding to marry. You could say something like the following to each of your children about how you hope to involve them as you build your life together:

> As your parent, I will always love you and want life's best for you. I hope that we will continue to have a close relationship and that you will accept this new person because she/he is important to me. The two of us love each other dearly and plan to get married. We'd like *you* to be a part of our new life together.
>
> I want you to know there is a "no compete" clause with your new stepparent in relation to your deceased/divorced parent. Your new stepparent is not a part of what happened. She/he does not want to replace your mom/dad but rather wants to develop a meaningful new relationship with you. Memories of your deceased parent or experiences with your divorced parent are separate from this new person whom I am bringing into your life. She/he is a totally new person in the family who will hopefully enhance your life even further.

These kinds of statements are aimed at helping you lay a healthy foundation on which to build a respectful, reciprocal relationship.

What Will the Kids Call Me as Their Stepparent?

What the kids will call you as a stepparent can be tricky, especially if you have dependent children in the home. Technically mothers and fathers are defined by the biological connection they have with their children. But often adopted kids call their adoptive parents "Mom" and "Dad," and when we marry, many of us call our in-laws "Mom" and "Dad." If you have very young children, you can simply instruct them to call you Mom or Dad. You may find that your older stepchildren will be comfortable calling you that if the relationship develops in a healthy way. But remember, using those names denotes a special closeness to that person and means children have to find a way to make it okay to have that close of a relationship with you. A sense of loyalty to or memories of their deceased or divorced parent may be too big a barrier for some children (both young and adult), particularly if they have not worked through their grief, and they will then want to call you by your given name. We suggest you let the children know your preference of what you would like to be called, but give them options so they can choose a way to address you that is comfortable for them. You may be a very important person in their life, but more like a friend or adult model than a "parent." Hopefully they will at least grow to value and appreciate the benefit of having you as a stepparent in their life. And as your relationship develops and grows closer over time, they may be willing to call you by a more intimate name if you want that as well.

Part 2: Blending a Chunky Family with Young Children in the Home

Some of you may remember the TV program from the early seventies called *The Brady Bunch*. The program was promoted as the ideal blended family in which each partner brought three kids into the marriage, combining them into a seemingly wonderful, loving, happy family. Maybe you want to have a "Brady Bunch" experience as each of you bring your children under one roof. Beginning to establish daily routines, sharing bathrooms, finding closet space for clothes, learning new rules and procedures—all this quickly puts pressure and stress on the "Brady Bunch" mentality.

Who Sets and Enforces the Rules for Dependent Children?

If dependent children will be living with you, even if it is only for a weekend at a time in the case of a divorce, one of the first issues you will want to talk through is who sets the rules and who enforces them. Sometimes each partner decides and implements consequences for what is appropriate or inappropriate behavior for their own children. We don't recommend this approach since it often separates the parent and stepparent in the child or adolescent's mind in a way that disempowers the stepparent. That can be the "kiss of death" because you are giving your children the idea they only have to listen to their parent. This approach might also create some distance in your marriage. The closeness you are trying to develop as a couple comes by being "in this together" rather than using an approach that feels like single-parenting again. Being united as a parental unit is essential to navigating the blending journey and truly moving from "me" to "we" again.

In setting standards and enforcing rules for children living at home, make certain you both know what was expected of them prior to your marriage. Working from that perspective, you can then decide what the two of you will expect of them now regarding household chores, family time, and appropriate behavior in your blended family. Identify not only behaviors within the household but also what you expect regarding school matters (such as respect for teachers, finishing homework) and behaviors with friends outside the home. You will also need to decide as a couple how you will discipline infractions of the rules. Discipline should be appropriate to the infraction, be it not completing a household chore, failing to finish a school assignment, fighting with a sibling, etc. If you arrive at an approach with which you are both comfortable, you can individually manage issues as they arise, confident that your partner supports you even if she or he is not present. Remember that if changes are initially too drastic from what was previously expected, your children may feel threatened and blame the stepparent as the instigator. Hopefully, as the original parent, you will reinforce the fact that you and the stepparent have agreed on these standards together, and the two of you remain united in your position. Children and adolescents need to develop a respectful attitude for the authority of *both* the biological or adoptive parent and the stepparent. If that doesn't happen, the stepparent may feel minimized, disrespected, and frustrated, which in turn will inhibit the development of closeness within your new family as well as your intimacy as a couple.

When disciplining both your own and your stepchildren, keep these principles in mind:

1. Be supportive of your spouse in the presence of your child regarding his or her management of the situation. If you think you would have handled it differently, wait to talk it over until the two of you are alone.
2. Avoid saying anything negative about your partner in front of your child. This does not mean you can't listen to a child's complaint about how your new partner handled a situation, but avoid colluding with your child. After talking with your spouse about the situation, invite your child to talk with both of you about the problematic issue and determine an appropriate solution together.
3. Always present a united front as a couple. After getting all the information about a request from your child, let your child know you will talk with the other parent/ stepparent about the request privately before giving your joint response.
4. In the event you disagree as a couple about a consequence for misbehavior and can't reach a suitable compromise, consider allowing the biological or adoptive parent to make the final decision. However, evaluate the outcome of the discipline to see if the approach effectively extinguished the unwanted behavior or if you need to revise your approach.

What Role Does My Ex-spouse Play in Raising the Children?

If you are divorced and share custody of your dependent children, you will likely still have some contact with your former spouse. Maintaining a non-adversarial or civil relationship with your former spouse, if at all possible, is much healthier for your children when making decisions that affect them. People have long debated whether it is less stressful to raise dependent children after a parent dies versus when a couple divorces. One advantage a divorced couple might have is getting some relief from full-time child care if the ex-spouse properly observes child visitation times and is responsible in being with the child(ren) as the divorce settlement allows. Then again, if your ex-spouse is difficult to deal with, you may think being widowed would be an advantage. But if your spouse died, obviously the other parent is not there to assist with child care, and you have to parent on your own. If your marriage was conflictual, whether you were divorced or widowed, you now have the freedom to parent your children according to your own standards and values, free from the negative influence of a spouse.

Part 3: Blending a Chunky Family with Emerging or Established Adult Children

If you or your partner's children have already left your home (at least off to college or in their own apartment), you face a number of issues that differ from those faced by people who still have children living with them. Since most people's lives are full and busy, staying in touch with your adult kids, and they with you, can be a challenge because they no longer live with you. Children who are emerging or established adults may initially be supportive of the new person in their parent's life because they are relieved that their parent seems happy in finding someone else. But this sense of relief often gives way to a variety of personal concerns, such as: How will my relationship with my original parent change? What kind of relationship do I want to have with this new person? What is expected of me, and what do I do with my sense of loyalty and love for my deceased or divorced parent who now appears to be replaced? As the parent, you can help your adult children by talking openly with them about those anxieties. If they resist talking, help them find an adult mentor or a counselor with whom they can process their fears and concerns. Hopefully after they have talked with someone else, they may feel ready to speak more openly with you about their feelings.

If your adult children are in their late teens to late twenties, they are likely consumed with college life, planning a career, dating, selecting a life partner, and setting up a household. The primary focus is *not* on what is going on in their parent's life. This process of exploring and settling in is self-focused for good and healthy reasons.

Even if your children are in the middle adult phase of life, parenting their own children and/or advancing their careers can distract them from their parent's life. Because of this, they can easily avoid grieving the death of a parent or the divorce that split their family of origin. They have to face it only when they come "home" to your house and experience the absence of their other parent. It is also fairly common for young adults to feel some sense of responsibility in taking care of their surviving parent. So when you begin to date, they may initially be relieved that they no longer have to worry (though that isn't necessary or healthy) about your life and happiness. As your relationship becomes more serious, or you even remarry, your emerging adult children may have quite a different reaction. They may miss their other parent all the more, or feel that you have abandoned the family of their childhood. They may have falsely assumed that while your life would take a new direction, their life was going to stay the same. Obviously that cannot be so. Change happens with death or divorce. Even more change comes when you remarry because the family structure is completely redefined with the addition of a stepparent. They may even hold their new stepparent responsible for all the unwanted changes happening in their family structure. The hope is that adult children will realize the benefits of having both their own parent and a stepparent (with all that person has to offer) as part of this newly formed family.

What follows are four reminders of what to do if you have adult aged children when blending your families:

1. Be intentional about planning events that will advance the blending process. We believe that the primary responsibility for setting the pace and planning activities rests with you and your new spouse. Realistically, adult kids do not invest as much interest in this new family, at least initially, nor do they have the knowledge and understanding, time, or energy to do it. As the years pass, however, you may be able to become less responsible for planning family activities. Hopefully the members of your new family will begin to suggest ways to get together as well. Obviously, each one of your kids (and their families, if they are married) is free to participate or not. Hopefully they will grow to understand that being connected and doing things together brings closeness. Continue to stress the importance you feel of having the blended family together, but needless to say, the level of your adult children's involvement is up to them.

2. Present a united front as a couple. Because of the temptation that many adult children may have to primarily continue a relationship with their own parent and perhaps even marginalize their new stepparent, try hard to employ a team approach with your kids. For example, it may help for both of you, at least initially, to be on the phone together when you call, and both of you participate in writing emails, cards, and letters and sign them together. That doesn't mean you can never contact your children without your partner (or them, you), but the healthy underlying message needs to be that you are a couple and would like them to accept

both of you on an equal basis. Having the opportunity to talk regularly with a stepparent helps to strengthen the relationship.

3. Blending takes time, energy, physical presence together, openness, and caring. We believe that if you want your two families to get along and do things together, you need all the ingredients we talked about above. The larger the number of adult children (and their families) and the greater the geographical distance between family members, the bigger the challenge you have in gathering everyone together. But remember, unlike dependent children who will live with you and can't avoid the reality of your new marriage, emancipated adult children are helped by structured and intentional time with you as a couple and with the rest of the blended family to become more comfortable with the "new normal" and develop a sense of being "family" together.

4. Blending two different family systems involves a number of considerations. On the one hand, you will be attempting to blend children and a parent of one family with children and their parent of another. You will read in the next chapter about some of the challenges this can present. Also, as a parent and stepparent you are attempting to develop individual relationships with each child as well. Both of these aspects of blending need attention if the process is to go forward effectively.

We do want to remind you that if your kids don't want to join in the blending process, it can feel like you are banging your head against a brick wall. That is sad because they are in fact choosing to distance themselves from their new family. But hopefully they will eventually realize they are missing out on the joys that a healthy blended family can offer. We hope that the next chapter, in which we tell the story of our own experience, will actually flesh out these points and give further direction for your own blending.

my spiritual journey while parenting and stepparenting

What does the Bible teach about "being family" together?

Once we saw a cartoon depicting a "family" picture at a wedding. A massive group of people were gathered at the front of the church. To the right side of the groom were his own divorced father and mother, new stepmother, several siblings along with two stepbrothers, one stepsister, and the previous father-in-law of the groom. On the bride's side was a similar conglomeration of people with various connections to the bride. The caption beneath the cartoon was simply "Our New Family."

Long gone are the days when we could assume that "family" meant a biological grouping of two married individuals and their children. Biological definitions don't work well today. "Family" can be whatever we want it to be.

The Bible suggests a different definition of "family" as belonging to the family of God. Those of us who are Christian are actually brothers and sisters in Christ.

So what does the biblical model of family tell us about being family together? How can we develop healthy family relationships especially when we are blending two families into a new one? First, recognize that Christ is the head of your new family. Developing consistent and shared faith values and making a joint commitment to follow the Bible's teachings are the first steps in building a healthy family system. Understanding the role and power of patience, kindness, forgiveness, and graciousness is important in redefining your new chunky family.

Second, know that the Bible tells us to love even our enemies, to practice hospitality to strangers, and to be kind to the fatherless and the widowed. The principle underneath these teachings is that it is Christianly possible to love "unlovable" people and develop healthy relationships with those to whom you might not be naturally attracted. Your new partner's children may sometimes seem more like adversaries, or at least strangers. But that is all the more reason for you to reach out to them as members of the body of Christ.

Finally, know that love in the Bible doesn't just happen. The verb "love" is often used as a command, something that happens with deliberate intention. Even when you are not inclined to love your stepchildren (or your own biological children for that matter), or they you, you still have within you the power and ability to love them graciously with Christian love. The words of Paul in Ephesians 4:15–16 might apply well here. "Instead, speaking the truth in love, we will in all things grow up into him who is the head, that is, Christ. From him the whole body, joined and held together by every supporting ligament, grows and builds itself up in love, as each part does its work." These words apply not only to the church but may also be used for growing a new family together. The emphasis in this passage is on the ligaments that hold the body together. In blending a chunky family, those ligaments are all the Christian virtues and behaviors that we use to blend the family together—the ligaments of respect, honesty, caring, patience, and the like.

What are the Christian characteristics of being a healthy (step)parent?

The Bible doesn't provide a section entitled "Ten Easy Steps for Effective Parenting or Stepparenting," but it does tell stories about both healthy and unhealthy parenting practices. It also provides principles to follow, but each one of us must make practical application of these principles to our own situation.

One general phrase we often use as a psychologist and as a pastor is that children and their offspring are an investment in a future we will not fully see. The saying is reminiscent of the fifth commandment in Exodus 20, for if our children learn to honor their parents, then God's lovingkindness will be passed on to the third and fourth generation of those who love God. So what principles of parenting and stepparenting can we derive biblically?

Be a MODEL. You can use the term "model" or "example," but the fact is that our children, adolescents, and adult children watch our behavior closely. A good parental model provides a picture of what a healthy Christian life looks like within your new emerging family system. Especially as a stepparent, modeling Christian behaviors and virtues can be a powerful step in building a relationship with your partner's children.

Be a MENTOR. A mentor is one who finds occasions to verbally explain to stepchildren the reasons why you behave the way you do, and why you expect certain things from them. Those explanations begin with our children. Do things in such a way that your children and stepchildren will want to know the motivations behind your healthy actions, and hopefully they will emulate them.

Be a MEMORY BANK. Help your children understand that rules, rituals, and routines within the family all have a history. The response to a child's, adolescent's, or adult child's question "why" should never be simply "because I said so." You need to examine what actually gives rise to some of your rules and practices as parents so that you can honor your children and stepchildren by giving an explanation. You are in the process of building their own reasoning ability and memory bank for future generations.

Be a MOTIVATOR. Proverbs 22:6 says, "Start children off on the way they should go, and even when they are old they will not turn from it." Be an encourager, an affirmer. Verbal rewards (words like "thanks," "glad you tried," "you really put forth a good effort") go miles toward building self-esteem and confidence. Be careful to affirm efforts, not necessarily end results. They may not have gotten the highest grade or even finished the race, but affirm the effort, the willingness to try.

Be a MANAGER. As parents of dependent children, you are able to establish some structure and appropriate authority within your family system. You are the parent, they are the child or adolescent. You are the model and mentor, they are the protégé or learner. Children need structure in which to grow and develop. You provide the scaffolding for them as they progressively build their lives. Eventually the scaffolding is removed, but if you have done your parental task well, the "building" of their life, complete with healthy self-esteem, assertiveness, and boundary development, will hopefully stand the test of time.

One final word about parenting is appropriate. Remember that parenting is a matter of influence, not control. You can do your best, but you can't guarantee the outcome. Hopefully your efforts will reap excellent benefits. But if that doesn't happen, be careful not to blame yourself. You have done what you can. If your stepchildren (or children, for that matter) are resisting you, then we urge you to read the next meditation as well.

What can I do as a Christian if my stepchildren don't accept me?

When you were young you may have played a game pulling off the petals of a flower, saying "he/she loves me, loves me not, loves me, loves me not" until all the petals were gone. The desire to be accepted and loved is a natural, God-given desire. Being ignored, or even worse, rejected, can be a blow to your heart and ego. The stakes go way up when we're talking about trying to build a relationship with your new (or future) partner's children. If you are at the point of getting engaged or are already remarried, you will want to have a sense of connection, caring, and love between you and your stepchildren. Anything less may seem as if they have rejected you, and this may create conflict or tension between you and them and possibly with your new spouse.

So what do you do if your partner's children don't espouse undying love and admiration? Even more pointedly, what if over the months of your courtship and even the early months of your marriage, you are met with some underlying resistance or even outright opposition or hostility? Along with good mental health management, which we have discussed, does the Bible give any suggestions on how to handle this?

While the Bible may not give any specific examples of step-children resisting the entrance of a stepparent into their life, it gives plenty of examples on how to deal Christianly with opposition and rejection. Let's go to Jesus in the Garden of Gethsemane. All those who had sung hallelujah just a few days before at his triumphal entry into Jerusalem had already left him. His disciples were asleep, insensitive to his agony and what lay ahead. Jesus wrestled with his Father concerning what he was about to face but concludes his prayer with the phrase: "Not my will but yours be done." This isn't sour grapes or passive resignation to the inevitable. To pray the prayer Christ modeled is an honest recognition that we do not control the outcome. To pray "your will be done" doesn't mean that God *wills* one's stepchildren's opposition or rejection. That is not the case any more than God *willing* that Adam and Eve disobey him or *willing* that the whole world be broken by sin, opposition, and rejection. However, that temporary rejection was an essential step toward the remedy for the brokenness that only Christ could provide. The final healing of that brokenness comes only with his return at the end of time. Between his resurrection and his return, we still pray "your will be done" as an acceptance that the world and all our relationships will never be perfect until life is shared together in heaven.

Nor does praying "your will be done" mean that you sit by passively waiting for God to do something. "Your will be done" really should be restated as "help me do what you want me to do, and work in the children's hearts and lives as well." God sees the big picture; each person only participates in a small part of the story. But that means you need to do your part as well. Jesus is the model of how you can manage the possible resistance of your stepchildren.

Remember the garden led to the cross. God's "will" required Jesus to move headlong into the opposition and rejection. The principle here is that you have to move into the pain not away from it in order to endure and conquer it. When you experience opposition from your stepchildren, remember that this is also a component of the grief journey. The old way of life is no more. Family life will be different. And even as exciting as your life with your new partner may be, opposition from her or his children is a reminder that you still need to build a "new normal" with them as well, and that doesn't happen overnight.

Then use this opposition for the greater good. Just as some self-defense techniques use the energy of the opposition to turn it into something good, you can attempt to do that with your stepchildren. Jesus, in dying on the cross, actually became victorious over the opposition that put him there.

Finally, keep the "long view" in mind. Breaking down the resistance and opposition may take a seemingly long time. You may not even be able to ever do it completely or as satisfactorily as you would like. On the other hand, persistence and patience often pay off in the end. Jesus could see the "long view"—the joy of victory. Daily or immediate resistance can be managed if you are able to keep the long-term vision of your family in mind. Pray for patience and wisdom. These are God's gifts to you as you press through to help structure your "new normal" family.

7

in our own words

A Sequel to "Blended or Chunky"

In the preceding chapter, we outlined the issues and approaches you might consider as you work toward blending families following your remarriage. In your household you may find little resistance and high levels of cooperation. However, numerous families face an uphill battle. Remember each couple's experience is unique in dealing with their children and stepchildren.

This chapter is in a format similar to that of chapter 5 but with the focus now on the blending of families after remarriage. As widowed persons who were remarried, we, along with our children, contribute our perspectives. Ed and Jean also share their experiences of blending their families after being divorced. We hope these stories give some insight into what your journey may be like and help encourage you along the way.

Through Our Eyes as Widowed

Susan's Perspective on Blending from the Time of the Marriage On

"Our wedding was a family affair with each of our children and my parents taking part in the ceremony by standing up with us and doing some of the readings. My daughter, Sarah, and Bob's son, Brian, each gave a toast at our wedding reception. We thought it was a wonderful day and a great start to our new life together. You have already read (maybe with a chuckle because it was a bit out of the box) about our invitation to bring our families with us on a portion of our honeymoon.

"As I look back, I would say that the hardest part of the blending process was that our kids were scattered across the country. That made it difficult to get us all together except for special occasions. I realize that when the children no longer live in the same home as their parents, getting to know their new stepparent and stepfamily is especially difficult. When Bob and I were engaged, I invited both of my stepdaughters to lunch separately to get to know each one better. I think I am a warm and caring person and tried to emulate that and show interest in their lives. Because my stepson, Brian, lived out of state, I didn't have much one-on-one time with him. Our times together were shared with his dad and me, and after Brian got married we included his wife as well. Now, at this point in time, our level of closeness with each of our adult children and their spouses varies depending on the amount of contact both we and they initiate with each other.

"We have attempted all along the way to make time for each of our children (and their families). We still try to do something special with the entire family during holidays and on other special occasions. We also take each family of grandchildren for a weekend at our parents' condo on Pentwater Lake, which flows into Lake Michigan. However, we both have worked full-time (Bob just recently retired) and are also very busy speaking at conferences, conducting workshops, and working on our writing projects. Our lives often feel to us like a juggling act, trying to build relationships within our family while each of us were pursuing our own professions. In addition, we feel a passion and calling to assist dying and grieving individuals and their caregivers through our speaking and writing endeavors.

"I must say, however, that I have been blessed throughout this entire process. My expanded blended family has enhanced my life. All of my stepchildren and their spouses and families are very special to me in their own unique ways, and I think I have a good relationship with them. I have learned how difficult blending can really be. I tend to be somewhat idealistic, and as a psychologist I often see a number of ways to make things better in people's lives, including my own. But the work of blending takes a lot more time and effort than I thought at first. I have a new appreciation for the complexity of two previously established family systems coming together. I believe I have grown in patience, grace, forgiveness, and acceptance. I think this experience has also made me more sensitive to the challenges other people face on their journey of blending."

Bob's Perspective on Blending from the Time of the Marriage On

"As I look back, I smile at how smoothly the wedding events went and how much fun we all seemed to have. We still have a portrait of our newly blended family above our fireplace that was taken on our wedding day. Over a decade has transpired, and I realize how little I knew about what lay ahead of us in bringing our families together.

"Actually, I'm not sure I can identify the hardest part of this process. Some of the blending went well—we all seemed to have a good time together. On one of the first Christmases during a family gathering near a ski resort, all of our children were outside at night playing football in the snow by the lights of their cars. That seemed to be a good omen of their getting along.

"The styles of our two families differ in terms of the normal depth of relationships they were accustomed to. Susan's family is, by its very nature, much more family oriented and connected. As my children were growing up, we certainly believed we were a close family. But now that I have experienced the closeness of Susan's family, I think I have a deeper appreciation for what a family can be. I am also more aware that I never developed the kind of closeness and intimacy with my own siblings and parents that Susan had and continues to have with her parents. I began to realize that there is so much more to a family than I experienced, and I began to expect behaviors from my children that they had never experienced or been exposed to.

"I was aware in developing a relationship with Susan's daughter, Sarah, that she was initially wary of me—not quite sure what to make of this new man in her mother's life. We went out for lunch a couple of times together. Sarah had already learned to be honest and direct in talking about her impressions, values, and goals. That made it a lot easier for me. I tried to make myself available as an adult listening ear as she went through college, got her first teaching job, and eventually married. Over this entire process, I believe she has come to see me as a valuable person in her life. We have developed a very close adult-adult relationship. She actually asks for my opinion on various matters and seems to value my input. She occasionally refers to me as 'Dad,' and I am delighted that we have developed such a level of closeness.

"Have there been some benefits to this blending of families? Absolutely. I now have another very special daughter and son-in-law and two more wonderful grandchildren. I have learned a little more about how to relate to my own biological children more authentically. One other advantage for me was that blending also included Susan's parents. My own father and mother died several decades ago, and now I have two parents who genuinely love and care about me, and I them, and I love that!"

We so badly wanted our kids to accept and love us and like their new siblings that we maybe tried too hard on occasion. We didn't think so at the time. But as we now hear some of the comments our kids made, we wonder how it would have turned out if we had not been so intentional in the early phases of blending. We fear that if we hadn't exerted a great deal of effort, our kids and their families would be in "separate pots" rather than the chunky blend we now have. We operated on the principle that once we were married we really didn't want a "your family" and "my family" who did things separately. We wanted "our family." So we arranged activities that we thought would begin new family traditions or simply be fun experiences. We organized a trip to an amusement park, had family gatherings at the beach, tried to create special holiday celebrations, hosted winter snow activities, and did anything else that qualified for what we at first called "blender bashes." In these events we tried to include our emerging adult children, their spouses or significant others, Susan's parents, and now our grandchildren. We used this approach from the time we were engaged through all of our thirteen years of marriage. We think that parents need to take the lead in bringing the two families together. As time went on, we altered our approach by letting them know what we'd like to see happen, hear their feedback regarding our proposals, find a compromise if possible, and then try to accept their individual levels of interest and investment. While on this journey, we continue to be reminded again and again that relationships are not perfect in any family, but we believe that two separate families can grow together more deeply and more lovingly when they spend time together with purpose and caring.

Their Kids' Perspectives on Blending Their Families

Since we were so intentional about bringing our families together, we wanted to know our children's perspective on the blending process, especially now that we have been married for thirteen years. So we asked: *What was the hardest part for you in blending our families? How could that have been better for you?*

For Sarah the hardest part was "trying to get to know the other kids with so many miles separating us. I feel like I missed out on having sibs my entire life as an only child, so I was looking forward to having some. With time, I realized that we are close but not like I pictured sibs to be. It isn't because I don't like them; I do. It is just hard to have a close relationship with someone you see only a few times a year."

For Carrie the issue wasn't just the geographic distance but the distance created by the two different family styles. She said: "I believe that when two parents try to blend their families, they need to consider that the two families grew up differently—different values, different traditions. One stepparent should not expect the stepchildren to accept his/her traditions and values."

We certainly agree that in blending, the couple must consider the different values and traditions of each family. However, the purpose of "blending" is to find a way to compromise, adapt, or accommodate to various aspects of each of these traditions as a framework in which to develop new family traditions. This is the essence of blending, with the hope that all members of the two separate families will participate in the process and see the value in finding new ways to be together.

The issue of maintaining a vital and close connection with their own parent seemed to be a big issue for Bob's daughters. Both Carrie and Christy, especially in the beginning, seemed to miss individual time with their dad. They felt like they lost the access they had to him before. Christy speculated, "I don't know if it was because he was the dad, and I was the daughter. I know that Susan still took the opportunity from time to time to do things alone with her daughter. I know that the dynamics are different when a child loses a mother versus a father and whether the child is a son or daughter. As far as blending the families as a whole, Dad and Susan have made many great efforts and have been very generous in providing opportunities for us to get close. I think their intentions were good, but sometimes things could have been allowed to develop more naturally."

Brian's response combined both themes of geographic distance inhibiting a closer relationship with his stepsibling and the change in relationship with his dad that seemed to occur when we married. He wrote: "By the time dad and Susan were married, I had already been overseas, moved across the country, met Marcia, and established a new life. I noticed changes in my dad. I noticed how his priorities, preferences, friends, and even his political party affiliation had changed. One of the hardest things for me was I felt like I lost the ability to talk with my dad one-on-one. At first, I really felt that it was an 'all or nothing' deal when talking with both dad and Susan, and I wanted to just talk to my dad. Today I feel like I can talk with either one of them individually if I feel a need to do so."

After responding to the hardest part of blending, we hoped our kids would say something positive about how our new family came together. So we asked them: *Do you see any advantages or "blessings" that have come from being in a blended family?* Their responses were all rather short but with various degrees of affirmation. Brian said rather directly: "The obvious blessing is that Dad and Susan had a new lease on life, and I have met some wonderful people." The other two followed the same theme, with Carrie sharing: "I've been blessed with some new great relationships." Both Carrie and Christy also commented, "I think I also have been blessed with a better understanding of others who have experienced the death of a parent followed by a new marriage for the surviving parent." Christy added, "The blessing of blending a family gave me the opportunity to have relationships with people I would have otherwise probably never encountered." Sarah said rather profoundly, "The primary advantage was that I got a dad." It seems that a stepparent filled some of the holes left with her dad's death. That is what we had hoped for with all of our kids.

But what would have made the process go more smoothly? We realize we never do anything perfectly. We can always improve. So we asked: *What do you think we or you could have done differently to enhance the blending process?*

The responses returned to the difference of opinion between some of our kids and us in our attempts to guide the process of blending rather than letting the relationship find its own way. What seemed to be purposeful and intentional to us as the newly married couple seemed to be too planned at times for some of our children.

Carrie said: "I think the attempt to blend families was too intentional and forced. For me, I think a more casual approach would have been better. I can understand that when two parents remarry, their greatest wish is to have everyone fit together perfectly, and they want it to happen sooner rather than later. By the time Dad and Susan married, we were all independent adults, and it's not as easy to mold adults as it is young children."

Bob's children seemed especially affected by the degree of intentionality we used in the blending process. They apparently wanted the process to go slower or follow what they deemed to be a more natural course of letting it "just happen." Brian echoed his sister's viewpoint that we should not have been "so intentional about blending the family." He went on to say that "this point may be contrary to your beliefs of how blending families should happen, but I think it created some resistance (at least with me) that wouldn't have been there if the process had been more casual. On a couple occasions, I would have rather laid on the floor or let the conversation direct the next activity. This may simply be a matter of style for me. Actually, I sometimes thought that Dad and Susan were trying to reach a level of blending that was not attainable. I didn't expect to share the intimate details of my life with my new family whom I saw only occasionally during the year. This is not because I disliked anyone in my new family. I truly enjoy the times our blended family have together. But my point is that a relationship with my stepsister and new grandparents will not be like the relationship I have with my sisters."

Sarah was more modified in her response but she did suggest a little less structure when everyone was together and more occasions early on with her mother in a one-on-one relationship. She wrote: "Mom, I think you tried too hard to involve Bob in our mother-daughter relationship. There were times when I just wanted to talk with you on the phone and do things with you alone. I loved spending time with the three of us, but I felt like our time sometimes became Mom, Bob, and me time instead of mother and daughter time."

In reading these comments, you can likely discern that we planned and organized the times when everyone gathered for a holiday or special occasion. We thought having some ideas of things we could do together would be of some benefit because of the number of people involved. Obviously, some of our children thought letting things evolve more spontaneously had greater merit. Even though we are delightfully happy in our marriage and never regretted the decision to marry for one second, at times blending our families continues to be a big challenge for us. Our blending is an evolving and dynamic process that will undoubtedly last our lifetime as we and our children and their families continue to change over time and as we relate together in a variety of ways.

We were interested to know what our children thought their life (or ours) might be like if we had not gotten married. So we inquired: *Do you think it would have been preferable for your parent to have remained single? What would be the advantages or disadvantages?*

Sarah cut to the heart of the issue, saying quite directly: "No. I am thrilled that my mom found someone to love and to love her back. She is the happiest I've ever known her to be. I admire their relationship, and I feel blessed to have Bob in my life. I can't think of any disadvantages at all."

Bob's children echoed some of Sarah's sentiment. Christy said, "I don't think that remaining single would have been an advantage for Dad. He seems happy with the way his life is going, and I believe that the accomplishments he and Susan have made together professionally have been great. They have enjoyed traveling together and having adventures that he probably would never have had if he had remained single."

Brian added, "This one is easy. No, it would not have been preferable for Dad to remain single. He would have been miserable. The advantage of him staying single would have been the fact that I wouldn't have to share him with anyone else. If I was the one who could have made the decision, I would have chosen for him to remarry despite the blending growing pains."

Carrie made a distinction for herself in saying that, "It was more beneficial for my dad to get married than it was for me to have him get married." How well adult children adjust and accept new situations in their lives obviously depends on many individual factors. One of the essential ingredients for a healthy adjustment toward accepting a "new normal" is the ability to put the relationship with their deceased parent in the past to make room to move on.

Both from our experience and our professional knowledge and practice, we realize that adult children's grief following the death of a father or mother takes a different form than what we experienced with the death of a husband or wife. We framed a question to them within the context that children of all ages tend to grieve intermittently over a longer period of time as they experience milestone events in their life versus the surviving spouse who grieves much more continually, usually over a two to four year period. We posed our questions to them by inquiring: *Where would you say you are in grieving your parent's death at this point? How often do you think about your deceased parent, and how often do you feel sad and miss him or her, if at all?* Their answers were candid and supported the research suggesting children (including adult children) grieve developmentally.

Listen to what Brian had to say: "I don't really like this question since it makes it sound like I woke up one morning and decided I was done grieving. I remember on the tenth anniversary of my mom's death I cried like a baby for a long time. I hadn't done that in years. Where am I now? No clue. I haven't wallowed or been depressed over her death in a long time, but I think of Mom a lot. I probably think of her in some way every day whether it's remembering that she died or wondering what she would think about a certain situation in my life."

Sarah was equally as candid about her experience grieving her father's death. "I can get emotional about it if I dwell on my feelings. I miss my biological dad and the relationship we might have if he were alive. I don't grieve his death anymore. At times when I'm down, I may feel sorry for myself and for him. It is hard to say how often I think about him, but when I'm in Michigan, I think of him more than when I am in Atlanta. Sometimes TV, radio, pictures, and seeing my kids with my husband tend to make me think of him. It isn't always sad thoughts. It's just remembering him."

The parental bond is strong and often does not significantly diminish emotionally with death. Often children have a difficult time thinking about the negative aspects of their deceased parent. If they tend to remember only the good things about the parent that died, it makes it almost impossible to get through the grief process. The stepparent is challenged to develop a close relationship with stepchildren independent of the deceased parent while still respecting the emotional bond with that parent. Of course, a healthy stepparent perspective is that he or she will never replace the deceased parent, because no one can ever replace another person, but they can become a significant and close person in their stepchildren's lives.

Christy and Carrie's responses almost echo each other as a classic example of recalling a deceased parent at milestone markers. Carrie said: "I think of my mom often but don't really feel sad when I think of her. I miss our relationship and the close mother-daughter bond we had. There are certain major events in my life that make me miss her more, such as my wedding day, the birth of my children, and recently the death of my grandma. I've wondered what she would have thought about my boys and how she might have been a grandma to them." Christy added: "My mom was an integral part of who I am, and I am sad that my children never got to meet her. But I think of her with happiness and how she would have been proud of me and my family."

This is our story. We are nowhere close to the end of it. Life is dynamic, and relationships continue to grow or diminish through varying circumstances and situations. The path toward a close, highly functional, "blended" family is a challenge. Notice the word *challenge* rather than *problem*. We choose to look at the reconstruction process in positive terms, but it is tough work. Hopefully you hear in our story that the blended family will never be the same as the original family might have been had the spouse/parent not died. However, with love, intentionality, time, patience, and room for individual personalities, a healthy new chunky family system can emerge. Hopefully you can find encouragement, hope, and some direction within our story for your own journey.

Through the Eyes of the Divorced

Perhaps the biggest difference between widowed and divorced people attempting to blend their families is the fact that following a divorce the biological or adoptive parents are usually still available for an ongoing relationship with their children. Unlike with the death of a parent, which ends that ongoing relationship, children of divorced parents must now balance their time and emotional energy between two separate family units comprised of their biological or adoptive divorced mother and father and perhaps new stepparents.

We asked Ed and Jean to comment on the process they used in bringing their families together. As we mentioned before, Ed has two daughters and Jean has two sons and one daughter. When they first met, Ed and Jean lived in different cities with their children in different school systems. Here is their story in their own words.

Jean's Perspective on Blending Their Families

"At first we agreed to each live in our own homes until Ed's girls and my daughter finished high school. This went on for about six months, but it was expensive and seemed unnecessary. So we tried to figure out how to live together, all five of us somewhere (my boys were in college). After considering several options, we sold our homes and bought one together. This turned out to be a disaster, but we just kept plugging along. The hardest part of blending was bringing all these new people into one family and living together. It was quite overwhelming to have our personal routines disrupted. I was not prepared for what happened to me emotionally when one of Ed's daughters moved out. I really wanted his children to accept me as an important person in their lives. So I tried to accept them for who they were and tried to be supportive of them. I spent a little time with each one separately to build a relationship as a friend. I knew I wasn't their parent. I just really wanted to love them. I encouraged Ed to continue his relationship with them and spend time with them without me, but that didn't seem to happen. I also tried not to take their resistance toward me personally. Ed and I had such different parenting styles that his girls were unhappy. He has meant a lot to my children even though I tried not to push him on them. When we are all together somehow there seems to be a wholeness in the middle of it all, and that is really a blessing.

"Because I was divorced, there is also the issue of how my kids relate to their father. I have tried to be supportive of their relationship with him and keep my feelings separate. They know I believe they have a responsibility to maintain a relationship with both their dad and me. I don't fight over them at the holidays so they can hopefully feel relaxed."

Ed's Perspective on Blending Their Families

"After six months of being married but not living together, I just couldn't stand it. But this was also the hardest part of blending for me. I know that I put a lot of pressure on Jean to be a mom to my kids. This resulted in some resentment that lingers to this day between Jean and my girls. I tried not to put expectations on Jean's kids to respond to me as a parent. I cared about them without desiring anything other than the hope that they would like me in return. At this point I think I have a really good relationship with my stepchildren. They and their children are a huge blessing in my life, and they have all accepted me as a part of their extended family. We truly love each other."

Their Kids' Perspectives on Blending Their Families

At the time of Ed and Jean's wedding, Jean's sons Gordon and Troy had already moved out of the home. Jean's daughter, Lisa, and Ed's daughters, Reed and Lynn, were still in high school. Lynn opted not to participate in this book, and therefore did not respond to the questionnaire. Since we wanted to know what bringing two families together was like for Ed and Jean's kids, we asked: *What was the hardest part in blending your two families? How could that have been better for you?*

Lisa was candid, saying: "The hardest part for me was sharing my living space with another man and living with Ed's two daughters. I was envious of my brothers because they were away at college and didn't have to deal with the blending transition. Ed's two daughters didn't seem too thrilled that they had to move to another city and go to a new high school. The first year was tough, living together and going to the same school. I was very different from them, and at first we didn't get along. All I wanted was to live in my old house with just my mom and me. I don't know if there could have been a better way to blend the two families. I think my mom and Ed did a pretty good job. It just took a while to adjust to living with two other girls who were so close to my age."

Ed's daughter Reed had nearly the same response as Lisa. She wrote: "As I remember, this idea about blending our families was not really discussed. I don't recall my dad saying that I was going to have two new brothers and a sister my age. I feel that this whole transition was *way* too quick. Before I knew it, my sister and I were moved from our hometown where we had lived our entire lives into Jean's home with a whole new school three times the size of our old one, and a new family as well! Like, 'Here you go—have a great time with your new siblings.' I feel strongly that this whole process should have been gradual. Maybe a weekend together or a vacation or something to give us an idea of our new life. I know that if I had taken a tour of the new school I would never have made that move with grace. My dad and Jean both will tell you I was very upset about this ordeal, and I made it my personal mission to make their lives pretty horrible because of it. I was a very angry, emotional teenager."

Both Troy and Gordon had already moved out of the house by the time their mother married Ed. Gordon reflected what was likely the sentiment of both of them in saying, "This was not a huge issue for me because I was out of the house. My time at home with the blended family was limited."

Moving the girls into the same home with their recently married parents was obviously a challenge and a stressful situation. So we also asked: *Do you see any advantages or blessings that have come from being in a blended family?*

What could have been done to make the process go more smoothly?

Troy was quite articulate on this issue—even a bit philosophical. He said: "My life has been enriched and enlivened by the presence of Ed. In many ways he has provided a different picture of what a father can be while at the same time being a great friend. To make the process go more smoothly, I would have encouraged them to talk with us candidly about the tension and potential discomfort that blending two different families causes and ask us about how we are feeling in the process, allowing space for our confusion and anger. Blending a family is the ultimate stamp of acknowledging the grief in losing your original family even if the blending is going smoothly."

Reed recognized that positive things can come from negative experiences but not without some emotional cost. She said: "I feel that the whole thing went too fast. There should have been more of an introductory phase. I feel that my dad wanted this all to work so badly that he ignored the warning signs from my sister and me. When I turned seventeen, I left my dad and Jean's house to live with my mom. I just could not handle it. In doing this, I also left my sister behind high and dry. That is something I will never forgive myself for. I was very self-centered at that point and was not thinking about her needs. However, there are always blessings even in the most dire situations. I feel that my blessing is having more family. I love my new family now. But initially I pretty much disliked everyone. I feel that this situation has helped me deal better with changes in my own life."

Gordon and Lisa were both fairly pragmatic and straightforward in their responses. Gordon simply said: "The biggest blessing has been that my children have a greater number of cousins." Lisa added: "The real blessing from our blended family is the giving and receiving of love from others. My mom is so much happier with Ed. All I pray for is to have both my mom and dad happy in their new marriages."

As we mentioned, the challenge of blending families following a divorce means that a child now maintains some form of relationship with two separated parents as well as a new stepparent(s). So we asked: *How do you feel about trying to balance time with both of your parents and the new blended family on special occasions, especially around the holidays?*

Reed reflected on the extreme busyness that comes with this newly blended family. "Holidays are indeed very, very busy. Now that I am married as well, we usually have about six different places to be at Christmas. It's a bit insane, but Dad and Jean moved their party until after the holidays, making it easier for all of us."

Lisa sees the situation similarly in saying, "Balancing time with my parents and blended families is challenging. During the non-holidays, it seems to work and everyone is somewhat flexible. However, it's tough during the holidays. I try to please all my parents, and I want to be able to spend time with everyone. But not everyone's schedules connect with one another. Usually in the end everything falls into place and people are happy, but it's a juggling act."

Gordon and Troy kept the theme of busyness in the forefront. Gordon wrote: "We are constantly rushing, and I feel like it isn't as relaxing as it would be without so many people to see. This has gotten worse with the addition of our own children." And Troy remarked: "During the holidays I feel exhausted, and initially I was somewhat bitter. On some years it felt like navigating an emotional minefield. As adult kids, we were all stretched fairly thin for several years because of what everyone expected of us. In recent years it has gotten better because a system of rotating the holidays has been worked out. However, even though we all agree (for the most part) on these systems, there are still hurt feelings expressed sometimes subtly and sometimes overtly."

So we wondered about the continuing relationship with their own parents, and therefore asked: *Has your relationship*

changed with either one of your parents and, if so, how?
How has it been to spend time with each of your parents
with their new partners?

Gordon, who is now married himself, said: "My relationship has changed mostly with my dad. In my own marriage, I began to take on some of my dad's undesirable behaviors that he displayed toward my mom. I didn't even realize I was doing this. I had seen and experienced those all my life, and this was 'normal.' After realizing this, I was able to change my behavior for the better, and I learned how to communicate with my dad in a healthier way."

Lisa realized that a stepdad can be a very important and helpful person in her life. She wrote: "Every child has a different relationship and perspective when it comes to their parents and stepparents. Some may be closer than others. For me, my relationship with my mother has been very close, and because I have a close relationship with her, I've also formed a wonderful relationship with my stepdad. I consider him another father figure because he is so loving and kind, and he will do just about anything for his kids. Seeing him love my mother is one of the reasons why I love and respect him. My relationship with my own dad is getting better. I'm not as close to my dad as I'd like to be. I think we still struggle in our father-daughter relationship because we both have a different way of doing things. I've forgiven him since the divorce, and I am trying to move forward in my relationship with him and my stepmother."

On the other hand, Reed sees both of her own parents as separate entities now, different in many ways. Here is her response: "My mom is still single, and her life is way different from my dad's. I believe that both my parents are better off now than they were before. Now that I am an adult and know them as separate people, it's hard to imagine them ever married to each other."

Juggling, walking a tightrope, whatever metaphor you choose, building and maintaining a healthy and satisfying relationship for dependent and adult children with both parents and a stepparent is a real challenge. You can't expect the road to be smooth and easy. But hopefully Ed and Jean's story and the perspective of their children can shed some light and direction for your own journey.

Conclusion

These last four chapters have focused on the choice of entering into another intimate relationship, remarrying, and blending families with either or both dependent and adult children. We have dealt with some of the theory and practices in moving in that direction. We have also told our stories about the experience of bringing families together both as widowed and as divorced persons. If you are somewhere in that process, we hope that our stories help normalize the challenges you face and serve to encourage you.

We also realize that many people, once widowed or divorced, do not want to remarry or cannot find a suitable partner. If that is your situation and you have been reading these chapters anyway, you will hopefully have a better idea of the blessings and pains of remarriage and blending. We encourage you all to now turn to the concluding chapter. Whether you remarry or remain single, how do you approach the road ahead? What level of hope do you have for the future? How will you decide what the contours of your life will look like five or ten years from now? And if you have a good idea of what your goals might be, how do you go about pursuing them in a healthy and productive way?

8

embracing your past— empowering your future

The Art of Moving On

Gary's Journal: Reading through my earlier journals, I realized again how desolate I felt when Eleanor died; I felt so alone, so deserted. It seemed like someone had slammed the door on my future—there was nothing to look forward to. It's been over two years since she died, and I have really learned and grown so much from this difficult experience. The biggest insight and relief for me is that I finally believe I have a future, even though I really have no idea what it's going to look like. Some days the possibilities even look exciting to me now! The emotions and distress of grieving kept me from believing that could happen early on. But after traveling a really rocky road and arriving on smoother ground, I learned that I not only *could* move on—I *needed to* consciously make that decision. Was it tough? You bet it was! But it was also liberating. Now I realize I don't need to know all the details of what my future is going to be. I still don't think I ever want to remarry, and that's okay. I do know that I am now ready to dive back into living and see what the future has in store for me.

Stacey's Journal: I felt pretty wounded both before and after my husband walked out on me and the kids. I know now that I jumped into dating Ben too quickly after my divorce. I think I was trying to validate my own worth and find help in managing life without my husband rather than learning to rely on myself. I stopped seeing Ben after we had dated for about four months because I felt I was using him, and I am surprised at how much stronger and empowered I now feel being on my own. I've gone alone on several weekend trips. I learned to launch the fishing boat by myself. I landed a new job that was a promotion from my previous employment. I'm actually getting to the point where I think I can do almost anything. I like being "me." Sure, I regret that I won't have a good marriage with my ex-spouse. But maybe someday I might be able to have that with someone else. Ben really is a nice guy. Maybe I will give our earlier dating relationship another chance, but I know that this time I will come at it from a position of strength. Now I think I may *want* to date Ben, but it is great to realize I don't *need* him anymore!

Preparing for the Next Chapter

One thing is certain. Your life didn't end when your spouse died or your divorce was finalized. You are still here and are working hard at determining what is next. Change is your constant companion on your journey toward creating a new chapter in your life. It will be different. After this devastating major life crisis, you are reconstructing yourself—no longer the same as before. You may not know what course your life will take as you develop it. But that's where faith and trust in a better tomorrow is so helpful.

The one main theme we have presented throughout this book is that in order for you to rebuild a happy and fulfilling life you need to be *intentional*. You, and only you, must decide where you are going from here. You know you can't go back to the old way, your "old normal," because that means your previous partner would need to reappear in your life, and you would have to revert back to how you used to be. At some point in your journey, you need to make a conscious decision to truly *choose* to live in the present and embrace the future, putting your life with your partner in the past and moving on by yourself. You have obviously traveled some distance from the end of your marital relationship, and you can now more likely appreciate the power of the journey metaphor for your life. You can see how far you have come, and can set your sights on the kind of life you would like for your future.

In this concluding chapter, we encourage you to do two things: first, learn from and use your past experiences to grow into a healthy, wiser person rather than living your life with regrets, anger, or a sense of failure. Second, we also want to encourage you to revisit the life goals you had before and during your marriage, deciding which of those plus new ones you wish to pursue for your next chapter.

Before unpacking this further, however, we want to reflect for just a few minutes on what you have learned about grieving as you moved through your grief. Hopefully you have embraced the premise of facing painful things as the only way to truly help you heal and move past whatever was difficult for you to do. For example, if you have been avoiding the pain associated with doing things like going to a favorite vacation spot or a family reunion without your spouse, you will want to revisit those painful areas to conquer them for yourself. After the death of your spouse or the breakup of your marriage, you need to have faced the pain of all the elements of your loss and have accurately assessed what you have learned in order to rebuild your life. Our hope is that you will realize the importance of being intentionally reflective about what you are learning from your past and deliberate about the choices you make regarding your future through this reflection process.

Being Deliberate about Learning from Your Personal Experiences

How do you become deliberate and intentional about learning from your past experiences? We believe the best way is to actively search your mind, heart, and soul, thinking about what you have learned. We think that writing these things down either by hand or computer is the best way to actually see and understand what has transpired in your life. We urge you to try writing or journaling even if you aren't someone who really enjoys writing. Some people find it easiest to write letters in their journal (that won't actually be mailed) to their previous partners and others who may be involved with some of the issues they have encountered on their journey so far. Whatever format you use, consider getting some type of journal to record your reflections on your experiences and what you have learned from them.

We suggest you use a four-step process in your journaling. First, describe an experience along with all your thoughts and feelings you have had on your journey from "we" to "me." Perhaps, as in the examples at the beginning of this chapter, you are struck by the differences in the thoughts and feelings you have now in comparison to what you had earlier in your grief process. You may be thinking something like: "I used to get angry a lot, but I find myself less inclined to lose my cool now," or "I felt overwhelmed at the prospect of being alone without my spouse, but now I actually look forward to my alone time." Perhaps you want to journal about something that still bothers you, such as: "I used to be more confident about doing things by myself when I was married. At least I knew that I had someone to back me up or affirm me when I began to question what I was doing. He died two years ago, and I still don't have the courage to do some of the things I had done before. We used to travel all over the US, and now I hardly dare go one hundred miles away from home by myself."

Second, make a value judgment about your management of the experience and your thinking associated with the issue you are journaling about. Is what you are saying a good thing for you? A not-so-good thing? You may journal something like "I think it's a good thing that I am not getting angry as quickly as I might have before." Or, "I think I need to be more confident being by myself so I can begin to do things I enjoy." And then journal ways you can increase your confidence about doing things solo. A step-by-step approach from a simple thing to a more difficult one will help you desensitize yourself and gain confidence bit by bit. Over time the process of journaling helps you see growth, and the issues you presently struggle with will eventually no longer be problematic.

Third, name the principle, truth, value, or belief that serves as the basis for your judgment. To say that something is good or bad, healthy or unhealthy, you have a point of reference in mind. Most of the time, the value will be pretty obvious to you. It is unhealthy to be angry or bitter all the time. It may even be wrong from the perspective of your faith belief or worldview. On the other hand, you likely think that it is healthy to be able to do things on your own rather than relying on someone else. This may be good in your estimation because you think that being self-sufficient is a healthier way to be in this world. As an example, you may eventually want to be able to go on a week-long road trip by yourself and think that would be a healthy and good thing to do.

Finally, decide how you are going to incorporate this insight into your life. Use your journal to write a specific plan of how you will accomplish your goal. Maybe you will want to try to be more independent doing things by yourself. So start small with going to a fast-food restaurant for lunch and progress to a table-service eating establishment. Then advance from going to a movie matinee by yourself to eventually a concert or a play. At that point, you may be ready for an overnight stay or a weekend trip by yourself even though you may be initially intimidated by the thought. Perhaps you will learn to so enjoy your independence that you resolve to make certain that if you ever do get into another committed relationship, that person must honor and respect your newfound sense of freedom to explore on your own terms. It is a wonderful feeling when you can manage and care for yourself largely on your own. Being needy isn't a healthy way to approach this new chapter in your life or to begin connecting with a new partner.

Setting New Goals for Your Life

We have been talking about determining your future goals and developing strategies to help attain them. But how do you go about deciding which goal or goals you would want to pursue? Are you going to change careers? If so, what kind of education or training do you need to acquire? Are you going to move to another part of the country (or world!)? What do you need to do to prepare for that? What kind of relationships do you want to develop and foster, and what are the best ways for you to keep friendships alive? Wouldn't it be better to just let life happen, to see what comes along? We think not. We believe being intentional and purposeful in your life is extremely important, something you hopefully learned on your grief journey following the death or divorce of your spouse. Now you have the opportunity and challenge to set your own direction in life. Do you want to remain single, date socially, or date seriously with the intention of eventually marrying again and, if you have children, blending your families? These issues all require a definite choice to engage in purposeful actions that lead in the direction of that goal.

However, sometimes your circumstances work against you. For example, you may want to remarry but can't find a suitable partner even though it was your goal and you had a specific action plan. This can be discouraging, especially if you really wanted an intimate partner again. But you can't always control the timing of achieving your goal, especially when it involves other people. A prospective partner may still appear down the road. Don't give up, but do reframe your desire so it's not your primary focus. This is somewhat like a couple having difficulty getting pregnant. Sometimes the harder they try the less likely they will get pregnant. But once they decide to adopt, you frequently hear that they have conceived themselves. Be intentional with your goals, but if you run into an obstacle you can't control, be flexible and adjust your goal to give yourself some latitude and time. We have found that when one door closes, another often opens at some point.

Keep in mind that goal setting requires two specific actions. One is to identify your specific goal (that which you want to achieve), and the second is to determine how you will attain that goal (the methods for pursuing the goal). Let's say that you want to make some new single friends. That's your goal. But how will you do that? Some people may take the direct approach by going to a social or dating website on the internet. Others may become involved in some type of activity that interests them and also involves meeting new people. Common interests (such as playing bridge, learning to do the swing, volunteering at a social agency, playing in a community band, or joining a ski club) often bring you into contact with people who can become close friends over time. Whatever your specific action plan, do know that as you become more invested in life, you will be more interesting and appealing to both yourself and others.

Remember that you are blessed with creativity and an imagination that you can use to achieve your new goals. Always be open to the surprise. Embrace the motto: "nothing ventured, nothing gained." Try different ways to accomplish your goals, and know that sometimes your goal may even change. Accomplishing one goal may lead to another that you never would have dreamed of or thought possible. Trust and believe in yourself, and you will be surprised at how many more doors open for you. Like yourself and practice healthy self-care. In coordination with that, work on developing a profound interest and consideration for others. Hopefully your future will be blessed with many new opportunities, joys, and growth along the way.

Another thing to review is your own deeper philosophy of life and your beliefs of why things happen. In other words, try to find some way to make sense for yourself of why this particularly difficult loss occurred in your life. Once you have lived through a significant life-changing experience like the loss of your spouse, your belief system needs to be reevaluated and either reconfirmed or readjusted. Our perspective is that eventually things can turn out for good, even though it may not look like it at the time. Regardless of what your religious belief or life philosophy is, you may be able to attest to the fact that good has come out of bad on occasions in your life. The death or divorce of your spouse was a bad thing—likely not what you wanted at all. But can you already see the sun shining on you again, see some evidence of new growth in you, and even surprise yourself in what you are becoming? Bad things that happen have a way of refining you and making you more complete, sensitive, and compassionate while being far more confident about your life. You can also become more resilient in facing whatever may come as a result of working your way through the death or divorce of your previous spouse.

Words for the Widowed

Two things happened to both of us as widowed persons when we emerged from our grief journeys following the death of our spouses. Independently we both discovered that we enjoyed the new sense of freedom and flexibility we had as a single, mature, and experienced adult. We both had very little opportunity prior to our first marriages to live as single persons. So being alone was initially a new and sometimes overwhelming experience. The second thing was that we discovered a number of activities and involvements we had not attempted before. We both traveled by ourselves to new places, even as we suggested you do. We both discovered that we could manage all the domestic responsibilities quite well. We learned to enjoy times of being alone. We made new friends. We became socially active. In time, we had a growing sense that we would be open to another intimate relationship if we met a person who fit our expectations and criteria—something we thought totally impossible earlier in our grief journeys.

So what does this mean for you as a widowed person? First, assess if you are through your grief. In our book *Traveling through Grief* we included a checklist of twenty-four items to help you know when you are through your grief journey.[6] These are based on the five goals of grief that must be completed before you are through the grieving process. If you have emotionally accepted the reality that your spouse has died, expressed all the emotions related to your loss, have moved your spouse into the past as a treasured and readily available memory, have redefined yourself with a new sense of self-confidence, and have reinvested in your life (incorporating both some of your former relationships and practices as well as developing new ones), then you are ready to move forward into the future.

If you do decide to date, make certain you can differentiate in your own mind between your former spouse and the person you are dating. You will need to relate to your date without confusing him or her with your deceased spouse. If, on the other hand, you are tempted to still make comparisons, inadvertently call him or her by your former spouse's name, or have experiences that trigger a lot of emotional memories of your life with your former spouse, you will want to press the hold button on any new dating relationship and first revisit and work on the suggestions we have made about getting through your grief following the death of your spouse.[7]

Words for the Divorced

Following a divorce, one's life is usually in turmoil for quite some time. You need to make a myriad of adjustments and thousands of decisions. So when we recommend that you become a reflective person and take time to journal, you might have earlier pushed that suggestion aside as being unrealistic and out of touch with what was happening to you. But hopefully now some semblance of stability is returning to your life. New routines are being established with your children and extended family. Your social life may be taking on a new pattern. So this is also the time to do the serious reflection on what you have learned from this entire experience. Many people who have been divorced are troubled by a nagging sense of personal failure. Have you dealt with this, if that was an issue? Have you identified as precisely as you can the behaviors or attitudes that you had in your previous marriage that may have contributed to its breakdown? Setting goals for the future, especially if you have some interest in dating and perhaps entering into another intimate relationship, depends critically on your level of honest, candid self-assessment. We hope you can apply the principles and techniques suggested in this chapter to your personal life so that you can set exciting, realistic, and attainable life goals for yourself in remaining single or deciding to date again.

my spiritual journey to embrace and empower

What does the Bible teach you about how to approach your future?

St. Gregory of Nyssa, a fourth-century bishop, said of Abraham that he left his ancestral home in response to God's call without knowing where he was headed—a sure sign that he was heading in the right direction. The same could be said of Moses, who was to lead Israel through the wilderness, or to the disciples when Jesus called them to "follow me." Your future may seem like a deep, dark mystery. You may have no idea which way you want to go. Choices! You have to make so many decisions, and how do you know which decisions are right for you?

Beginning again—having a second chance—is both an opportunity and a challenge. You have an opportunity to re-create your life with a shape and texture that are satisfying and rewarding. You also have a huge challenge because this endeavor requires a lot of hard work. What does the Bible teach us about how to approach the future? What will God do for you, and with you, as you try to put your life back together again?

First, remember that God is in charge. He is the leader. There may be times in your recent past when that didn't seem to be the case. A spouse dies, or you are divorced, and you may well have wondered where God was through that entire process. Just remember, God never promised that your life would be without trouble or hardship. On the contrary, he promises you strength and direction precisely because you will have trouble and hardship. Psalm 23 promises that "even though I walk through the darkest valley, I will fear no evil, for you are with me; your rod and your staff, they comfort me."

Second, your life is a seamless story in spite of this disruption. The divorce or death may seem to you like your life had taken a major detour—a major disruption. Suddenly it feels like whatever preceded this disruption is sealed off from whatever will follow. But that is not the case. You are still you. The God who watched over you as a child, an adolescent, an emerging adult, and into your adult years is the same God who is with you now. To you, this divorce or death may be the biggest life-altering event you will have to face. But to the Lord, none of these changes can disrupt his lordship and leadership of your life. He brought the Israelites through the Red Sea. He was able to raise Lazarus from the dead. He encouraged the early New Testament church through his Spirit to face unspeakable persecution. And through it all God remained his constant self, never changing, always gracious.

Third, God often leads in a direction you didn't anticipate. God overrules our sense of direction. He doesn't necessarily take the shortest route. But he will give clear and indisputable guidance. Even in his leading, God offers us options. He doesn't drag us around on the end of a leash, forcing us to obey his every command. Did you notice that one of the reasons God led the Israelites into the desert toward the Red Sea was that he didn't want them to flee back to Egypt if they ran into the Philistine army? They had to choose to follow his lead. Sometimes they did, and they were blessed. Sometimes they did not, and they suffered the consequences. We still have to decide to follow him. Being single again may seem like you are in the desert up against the Red Sea. But God is there with you. Through prayer, meditation, journaling, and talking with trusted friends and advisors, you may find that you have a number of creative options for reconfiguring your life that you had never considered before. Some options, now that you are single, may present themselves that would not have been possible when you were a married person. Consider every potential alternative.

Fourth, God allows you to hold your decisions lightly. The goal can be achieved through a variety of means, but the goal will be achieved. The Israelites did make it to the Promised Land. God gave them their inheritance. Sometimes they had to change their directions and their plans. What should have been a forty-day journey took forty years. The goal was not reached instantly. You have the rest of your entire life to work on this matter of following God's lead. You may well experience other detours, obstacles, and disruptions along the way. But God still leads.

Finally, when God leads, he accomplishes his purposes. His promises are sure. As Jesus and his disciples stood on the brink of his arrest, trial, and crucifixion, Jesus assured them that the future was held firmly in his hand. "Do not let your hearts be troubled," he said in John 14. "Trust in God, trust also in me. . . . You may ask me for anything in my name, and I will do it. . . . Peace I leave with you; my peace I give you. I do not give to you as the world gives. Do not let your hearts be troubled and do not be afraid." We hope and pray these words also encourage you as you face a future that seems mysterious, but a future held firmly in his hand. There is certainty with God through the uncertainty in your life.

notes

1. Susan J. Zonnebelt-Smeenge and Robert C. De Vries, *Traveling through Grief: Learning to Live Again after the Death of a Loved One* (Grand Rapids: Baker, 2006).

2. Richard J. Foster, *Freedom of Simplicity* (San Francisco: HarperCollins, 1981).

3. T. H. Holmes and R. H. Rahe, "The Social Readjustment Rating Scale," *J Psychosom Res* 11 (1967): 213-18.

4. We have changed their names and those of their children to protect their anonymity.

5. Adapted from a version found on ths.gardenweb.com on November 13, 2008.

6. Zonnebelt-Smeenge and De Vries, *Traveling through Grief*, 119-22.

7. You may be especially helped by reading our book *Getting to the Other Side of Grief: Overcoming the Loss of a Spouse* (Grand Rapids: Baker, 1998).

Divorce recovery support groups
www.divorcecare.org

Find help. Discover hope. Experience healing.

Divorce and separation leave a trail of devastation in the lives of those involved. The thought of picking up and repairing the broken pieces is overwhelming. Where to start? How could anything be made right again? How do I keep from being hurt even more?

DivorceCare support groups are comprised of people who know what it's like to walk that trail. At DivorceCare you'll find answers, encouragement, and the strength to move forward in a way that's healthy.

> *"It's been a huge comfort to walk into DivorceCare and meet people who understand where I'm at. I don't have to have it all together. I come as I am and they know what I mean." —Monica*

The weekly, video-based meetings provide wise counsel from Christian experts on topics such as dealing with emotions, what the Bible says about divorce, managing finances, reconciliation, and new relationships. You'll spend time discussing concepts from the video and how to apply them in your life. A short, daily workbook Bible study and journal will help you work through issues and see your situation in a more promising light.

To find a DivorceCare group near you, visit **www.divorcecare.org** and use the "Find a Group" locator. You may also call **800-489-7778** or email **info@divorcecare.org**.

Other helpful resources at **DivorceCare.org** include free daily email devotions, a personal Bible study, and a bookstore featuring divorce-related materials.

Help for your children

If you have children, they'll love **DivorceCare for Kids (DC4K)**, a fun-filled place for children ages 5–12 whose parents are separated or divorced. The games, music, crafts, and activity books help the children identify and cope with their emotions and communicate with their parents. Find a **DC4K** group at **www.dc4k.org**.

GRIEF SHARE®

Grief recovery support groups
Find hope.
www.griefshare.org

When someone you love dies, despair threatens to engulf you. The sadness may seem like it will last forever, but it won't.

At a GriefShare support group, you'll meet people who have an understanding of what you're going through—the exhaustion, mental fog, and emotional burdens—but who have discovered how to find peace in the midst of their pain.

*"The people I saw at GriefShare had a glimmer of hope …
I knew I needed it to survive." — Joanne*

Through the weekly, video-based GriefShare program, you'll learn how to identify and sort through your tangled emotions, where to find comfort and strength, and how to walk the journey of grief in a way that's healthy and will bring healing. The videos feature insights from respected Christian counselors, pastors, and teachers and personal testimonies from people who've experienced a loved one's death.

Through the video seminars, small group discussion time, and daily personal Bible study, you'll find out what to do with your questions "Why?" You'll gain practical advice on how to keep from getting stuck in grief. You'll also learn how to manage your grieving family, and how to handle people who think they're helping you, but aren't!

GriefShare groups are meeting across the nation and throughout the world. To find a group in your area, use the "Find a Group" search engine at **www.griefshare.org.** Or you may choose to call **800-395-5755** or email **info@griefshare.org.**

*Find additional healing resources at **GriefShare.org**: Free daily email devotions, a personal Bible study, and a bookstore filled with recommended grief-related materials.*